ADHD CLEANING HACKS

PROVEN STRATEGIES AND ACTIONABLE CHECKLISTS FOR A CALMER HOME AND MIND

CRAIG GORDON

© **Copyright 2023 - All rights reserved.**

The content contained within this book may not be reproduced, duplicated or transmitted without direct written permission from the author or the publisher.

Under no circumstances will any blame or legal responsibility be held against the publisher, or author, for any damages, reparation, or monetary loss due to the information contained within this book, either directly or indirectly.

Legal Notice:

This book is copyright protected. It is only for personal use. You cannot amend, distribute, sell, use, quote or paraphrase any part, or the content within this book, without the consent of the author or publisher.

Disclaimer Notice:

Please note the information contained within this document is for educational and entertainment purposes only. All effort has been executed to present accurate, up to date, reliable, complete information. No warranties of any kind are declared or implied. Readers acknowledge that the author is not engaged in the rendering of legal, financial, medical or professional advice. The content within this book has been derived from various sources. Please consult a licensed professional before attempting any techniques outlined in this book.

By reading this document, the reader agrees that under no circumstances is the author responsible for any losses, direct or indirect, that are incurred as a result of the use of the information contained within this document, including, but not limited to, errors, omissions, or inaccuracies.

CONTENTS

Introduction: The ADHD Mind in a Neat Home — 7

1. THE LANDSCAPE OF ADHD AND HOUSEKEEPING — 13
   ADHD Traits — 14
   The Housekeeping Challenge — 21
   Breaking the Myths — 24
   Case Study: A Day in the Life—ADHD and the Battle of Cleaning — 27

2. ADHD-FRIENDLY CLEANING APPROACHES — 31
   Why Standard Methods Fail — 31
   Tailoring to the ADHD Mind — 35
   Setting up for Success — 41
   A Failed Cleaning Experiment Turned Success — 46

3. ZONES OF IMPACT — 49
   Identifying Zones — 50
   Prioritizing Efforts — 55
   Rotation Cleaning System — 59
   Finding Peace by Addressing Just One Zone — 64

4. MAKING CLEANING FUN AND REWARDING — 67
   Gamifying Cleaning — 68
   The Power of Music and Podcasts — 72
   Group Cleaning — 76
   Turning a Dreaded Cleaning Day Into a Party — 81

5. OVERCOMING EMOTIONAL
   BARRIERS 83
   Identifying Blocks 84
   Reframing and Acceptance 87
   Seeking Support 92
   From Emotional Paralysis to Cleaning
   Empowerment 97

6. BUILDING AND MAINTAINING
   HABITS 101
   The Power of Routine 102
   Cue-Routine-Reward Cycle 107
   Addressing Slips 112
   ADHD and Habits: Two Cases 117

7. DESIGNING AN ADHD-FRIENDLY
   HOME ENVIRONMENT 121
   Decluttering 121
   Organizational Systems 126
   Minimalism and ADHD 131
   Case Study: A Complete Transformation ... 135

8. LONG-TERM STRATEGIES AND
   CONTINUAL GROWTH 137
   Review and Reflect 138
   Adapting to Changes 144
   Continual Learning 147
   A Lifelong Journey of Mastering Space ... 152

9. PRACTICAL CLEANING STRATEGIES
   TAILORED FOR ADHD 155
   The Living Room Retreat 156
   The 5-minute Living Room
   Transformation 160
   The Kitchen Conquest 161
   A Switch From a Chaotic Kitchen to a
   Culinary Haven 165

The Bathroom Battle	166
Case Study: The Magic of Routine in Maintaining a Sparkling Bathroom	171

10. THE DEEPER MEANING OF A TIDY HOME — 173

Beyond the Physical	173
Personal Growth and ADHD	177
The Broader Impact	181
Finding Inner Peace Through Cleaning	184

Conclusion: Embracing the Journey	189
Bonus Checklist: ADHD-Friendly Cleaning	
Checklist: Week-by-Week	193
References	199

INTRODUCTION: THE ADHD MIND IN A NEAT HOME

Would you believe it if someone told you that ADHD isn't a disorder—it's your superpower? If not, you should. With the right direction, you can turn everyday challenges into incredible opportunities through the power of hyper-focus and organization.

The ADHD brain is often misunderstood, but it's brimming with extraordinary potential. Rather than a *dis-order* think, *different*-order, a unique way of seeing the world. Yes, it gets heavy sometimes—you can't sit still, and your thoughts are too loud, but you can channel your energies with laser-like precision to transform your so-called weakness into an enviable strength. Just imagine a treasure trove of creativity, innovation, and untapped potential. It's about time we stop trying to fit your remarkable mind into conventional boxes and start celebrating your unique qualities.

The cluttered desk, the overflowing closet, the kitchen that seems to spawn dirty dishes faster than you can blink. It's exhausting, disheartening, and downright overwhelming. But it doesn't have to be this way. It's a common misconception that people with ADHD are inherently messy or disorganized, and it's simply not true. What's true is that, yes, issues with focus and attention make some people with ADHD struggle to stay on top of things, but it doesn't mean they can't maintain a tidy environment. In fact, many develop excellent coping strategies and organizational systems to counteract these difficulties. Let's not forget that tidiness isn't exclusive to those without ADHD—everyone struggles from time to time. What's likely to get you up and running, though, is knowing your ADHD brain is wired to use the right tools and strategies to leave these stereotypes in the dust. Want to know how you can use them in your quest for a neat home?

UNLEASH THE POWER OF ADHD IN HOME CLEANING

Not just a concept, the power of ADHD in home cleaning is a transformative lifestyle change, breathing new life into your daily routine and into your mind. Now, you might be thinking, *But I have ADHD—organization and tidiness aren't exactly my strong suits.* Well, let's set the record straight: Having ADHD does not mean you are inherently disorganized. It simply means you need something *tailor-made*, a system that works in harmony with your ADHD brain's potential, not against it. Why? Because it's not just about cleaning; it's about empowerment—taking ADHD challenges and transforming them into your greatest strengths. Tap into this power and you'll feel unmatched satisfaction and control, the pride of an organized living room, the pleasure of a tidy kitchen, and peace of mind from knowing exactly where your important documents are. This is the power of harnessing your ADHD brain in home cleaning. The amazing results from this journey are a testament to its worth because not only will your home be cleaner, but your life will be more organized, and you'll feel less stressed. And the beauty of it is that these aren't just temporary results.

Think about it—if you know why you can't keep things tidy and have specific strategies tailored for ADHD, how easy would it be to turn what seems like a mountain into a manageable molehill? In the simplest terms, you're going to learn exactly why your current methods aren't working for you. From there, you'll discover an arsenal of actionable strategies—tried and tested. We're talking practical advice *specifically* designed for the ADHD brain, giving you the confidence to grow personally by building consistent habits.

Don't just take my word for it; Sarah's home was her sanctuary and her chaos. She loved her space, but it was a permanent reminder of her ADHD—piles of clothes, unopened mail, and half-finished art projects. She could never find her keys or remember where she left her phone. Friends and family criticized her—"Sarah, why can't you just tidy up?" But it wasn't that simple. One day, Sarah stumbled across some ADHD cleaning hacks. Intrigued, she learned about the unique wiring of the ADHD brain, the constant mental chatter, and the struggle to focus. She realized her disorganization was a symptom of ADHD. Inspired, she took up the challenge of transforming her living space, starting small, setting a timer for just five minutes a day to declutter. It wasn't easy, but she kept at it. The smallest victories were worth the effort—a clear table, a neatly folded pile of clothes. As time went on, Sarah understood her ADHD better, and managing her home became easier by harnessing her unique strengths; her creativity sparked the design of aesthetically pleasing storage solutions, and hyperactivity made her an efficient and energetic cleaner. Sarah and her home were transformed—she found her keys where she expected them, her bills were paid on time, and all her art projects were stored neatly. Most importantly, she felt calm like she'd never felt before.

Sarah's story is a testament to the potential within each of us to overcome our challenges. Because it's not about becoming someone else or being perfect; it's about accepting who you really are, ADHD and all, and learning how to create a space that truly reflects that. In the end, Sarah's experience is more than just a tale of a woman with ADHD discovering her cleaning potential. It's a story of self-discovery, understanding, and empowerment—the realization to live beyond labels and embrace the unique strengths within each of us. If you've ever felt like your mess is pulling you under, unlock the power of your ADHD brain and use it to revamp your home cleaning. It's time to turn your "mess" into a "message" of strength, resilience, and triumph.

1

THE LANDSCAPE OF ADHD AND HOUSEKEEPING

Have you ever wondered why housekeeping seems like such a monumental task with ADHD? It's not laziness or a lack of willpower. Instead, it has to do with how your brain processes information and prioritizes tasks. ADHD comes with a side of hyperfocus, a condition where it's easy to get so engrossed with one thing you lose track of everything else. Now, imagine trying to do mundane tasks like cleaning when your mind is buzzing with a million more intriguing ideas. That's the daily challenge for people with ADHD. So, if your home is cluttered or messy, don't be so hasty to judge yourself—tidying up is a battle against the mind. Let's go a little deeper into the unique traits of ADHD and explore how they complicate simple chores like keeping a house clean.

ADHD TRAITS

ADHD isn't just about being hyperactive or easily distracted; it's a complex neurological disorder affecting how you process information and prioritize tasks. For you, tidying up isn't just a chore; it means organizing your thoughts, staying focused, and following through—things that don't come easy with the varying degrees of ADHD symptoms.

The ADHD Spectrum

The ADHD spectrum is fascinating because it's not a one-size-fits-all thing. Many symptoms are associated with ADHD, ranging from mild to severe, and they differ significantly from person to person. These symptoms are classified into three types (CHADD, 2018): predominantly inattentive, predominantly hyperactive-impulsive, or a combination of both:

- **Inattentiveness**: Difficulty maintaining focus, being easily distracted, forgetfulness, and struggling with organization and completing tasks. It's like your mind is a TV with someone else holding the remote, constantly changing the channel.
- **Hyperactivity and impulsivity**: Excessive talking, fidgeting, difficulty sitting still,

restlessness, and acting without thinking through the consequences. It's like having a motor that's always running at full speed.

Not everyone with ADHD will experience all these symptoms. Some might lean more toward inattentiveness, others toward hyperactivity, and others still might experience a mix of both. The severity of these symptoms also varies from person to person, with each distinct spectrum influencing their approach to housekeeping—especially if they get in the way of keeping things organized. Here's why:

- **Organizing and prioritizing**: You may not know where to start cleaning or how to keep things neat.
- **Sustaining attention**: You start one task, get distracted by another, and end up with a half-dozen unfinished chores.
- **Sensory sensitivity**: Certain chores, like vacuuming or washing dishes, get overwhelming because of sensory overload.
- **Forgetfulness**: You might start doing the laundry, get distracted, and forget to put it in the dryer or you might clean up a room but forget where you put things.

- **Impulsivity**: Being impulsive can lead to hasty cleaning decisions, like throwing away important items or cleaning without a clear plan.

There's more to coping with ADHD than adjusting to the spectrum; it also involves harnessing your unique strengths and managing the challenges that come with it. An everyday task can be a battleground or a triumph, depending on how you approach it.

Strengths and Challenges

Living with ADHD is like surfing on wild waves—thrilling, unpredictable, and a test of resilience. Yes, the challenges are real; the distractibility is frustrating, and the struggle with focus is like a relentless battle. But your brain's wiring allows you to think outside the box, innovate, and create. Yes, your attention might dart from one thing to another, but when you're passionate about something, you can hyperfocus like no other. Knowing your strengths and challenges can help you *tailor* strategies, like ADHD-friendly cleaning approaches, to leverage your potential, not undermine it.

Strengths:

- **High energy**: Imagine if you channel this bubbling source of energy toward the cleaning jobs around your home. Not only will tasks feel like less of a burden, but your infectious enthusiasm could also inspire others in the house to join in, making the cleaning process more productive and successful.
- **Hyperfocus**: The incredible ability to immerse yourself in a task is your secret weapon for tackling those deep-cleaning projects. When your hyperfocus kicks in, tidying up isn't just a chore but an engaging challenge you can master for a clean, organized space you'll love.
- **Creativity**: Use your unique perspective to find solutions others miss—you can devise innovative cleaning strategies, turning a mundane chore into an opportunity for creative problem-solving and expression.
- **Resilience**: Living with ADHD indeed presents challenges, but it also strengthens your character. Apply this resilience to your cleaning tasks, even when they *seem* overwhelming, and your determination to overcome hurdles will transform these challenges into accomplishments.

- **Spontaneity**: Not always a bad thing; spontaneity brings joy and excitement and adds an element of surprise to your life and those around you. Rather than sticking to a rigid cleaning schedule, give yourself the freedom to tackle a cleaning project whenever the mood strikes.

Challenges:

- **Concentration**: When it comes to cleaning, following through isn't so easy when you can't concentrate. If your mind is constantly shifting gears, you'll start multiple tasks but won't finish any of them, resulting in a chaotic, half-cleaned space.
- **Impulsivity**: If you make snap decisions like throwing out important items in a rush to declutter, you might regret it later. Similarly, stopping in the middle of a cleaning task to start another creates a house that's tidy in parts but, overall, still messy.
- **Restlessness**: Restlessness makes the calming, methodical process of cleaning feel like a burden. If you can't sit still and focus, you'll end up rushing through your cleaning routine,

which can lead to missed spots and an overall less tidy environment.

- **Organization**: What happens when you're unable to plan out your cleaning tasks or follow a systematic approach? Inefficient cleaning and poor time management—meaning cleaning takes longer than it should.
- **Memory retention**: Maybe you forget where you put things or can't remember if you've cleaned a particular area. When forgetfulness is an issue, misplacing cleaning supplies or failing to clean certain areas can lead to a disorganized and improperly cleaned space.

Now, let's look at the dual nature of distractibility, a common ADHD trait, and how it can also be a surprising strength.

The Double-Edged Sword of Distractibility

The distractibility trait of ADHD can be a double-edged sword. On one side, this trait is a unique strength. It fuels your creativity, encourages you to think outside the box, and opens your eyes to all kinds of new opportunities—your wandering mind isn't a flaw; it's a feature. But let's not sugarcoat it; the other edge of that sword is sharp. It's all too easy to get lost in a forest of fascinating thoughts and ideas only to realize you've strayed off the path. Tasks take longer, details are missed, and it feels like you're constantly playing catch-up. When we think about distractibility, we often consider it a hurdle, especially for people with ADHD. This perspective has merit because if you're easily distracted, then you can't concentrate or retain information very well. Unwanted intrusive thoughts, background noise, and external distractions compound these challenges.

Not all distractions are created equal—the same tendency toward distraction also leads to hyperfocus. This is where the flip side of the sword comes in. Hyperfocus is like being in a world of your own, completely immersed, and performing at your peak. It's an ability capable of extraordinary creativity, resilience, and productivity. To really wield this double-edged sword, you must understand it. By recognizing patterns of hyperfocus, identifying high-value tasks, and improving time management skills, you can turn distractibility into an asset. It's nothing to do with laziness or a lack of effort; it's simply how your brain is wired and is nothing to be ashamed of. Like any other skill, you can learn and improve by managing it and using it to advance to a cleaner home. How? Through understanding.

THE HOUSEKEEPING CHALLENGE

Cleaning is only one aspect of housekeeping. Other elements are organizing, maintaining, and managing a household. Now, imagine trying to do that with ADHD traits—those that affect the executive functions of the brain, responsible for organizing, planning, and prioritizing tasks. It's like trying to keep track of a hundred different things while juggling on a unicycle. Not easy, right?

When you're in a constant battle with housekeeping, have you ever stopped to consider why this clutter keeps piling up in the first place?

Why Clutter Happens

Imagine this: You've just got home after a long day at work. There's clutter everywhere—it's on the coffee table, the kitchen counter, and even the stairs. You ask yourself, "How did this happen?" Well, clutter happens when stuff gets scattered around:

- buying something on impulse without thinking about where it'll go
- postponing sorting through the mail instead of dumping it on the nearest flat surface
- having too much stuff lying around and not enough space to store it

So, clutter doesn't just appear out of thin air—it's the manifestation of delayed decisions, procrastination, and a lack of proper organization systems. When we don't have specific places for our items or an effective system set up, things end up in places they shouldn't be, thus creating clutter. With ADHD, the patterns of inattention, hyperactivity, and impulsivity make it challenging to control clutter.

Emotional Toll of Messiness

And then what happens? Your brain hits a wall, you can't focus, and your anxiety skyrockets. This is the emotional toll of messiness. There's more to a tidy home than aesthetics; a lot of it is about how our surroundings impact our mental health. With ADHD, your brain is already in a constant whirl of activity, and having to work through a messy environment adds an extra layer of stress and frustration. Messiness triggers overwhelm, anxiety, and even guilt (Stoler, 2023). It might seem like a trivial issue to some, but when you're in the midst of it, it's all-consuming. These feelings get even more intense because of your heightened sensitivity to environmental stimuli. The constant reminder of tasks undone is a burden no one needs to carry. Yet, this emotional weariness is just the beginning, as it sets off a relentless cycle of overwhelm, making you feel like you're constantly running behind.

The Cycle of Overwhelm

The cycle of overwhelm in a messy home is a vicious one. It starts with a small mess, grows into a large one, and then becomes overwhelming—the coffee table piled high with papers, unwashed mugs on the countertop, and dust everywhere you look. This is how it starts:

1. **Clutter accumulation:** You're paralyzed by the mess but also by the thought of having to clean it up. As tasks go unfinished, physical clutter builds up, leading to mental clutter, making it even harder to focus.
2. **The overwhelm sets in:** Eventually, the clutter reaches a tipping point and you're overwhelmed. You're stuck; the mess feels insurmountable, so you ignore it, hoping it'll somehow resolve itself. But it doesn't—each day, the clutter grows, and with it, your stress levels.
3. **Avoidance:** The more you avoid the mess, the bigger it gets. Your home becomes a visual representation of the anxiety you're feeling inside, which makes you feel bad.
4. **Ignoring the problem:** The cycle continues as you avoid dealing with the mess. You dread coming home, and the clutter spills over into

other aspects of your life. You can't relax, concentrate, or sleep. Your home, the place that's supposed to be comforting and peaceful, is now a major source of stress. And guess what? This anxiety further hampers your ability to concentrate, so you can't even begin to think about tackling the mess, so you avoid it, thus perpetuating the cycle.

This is the cycle of overwhelm, and it's a tough one to break. But don't worry, we're going to tackle it together. The first step? Addressing myths and finding ways to change your perspective.

BREAKING THE MYTHS

You've probably heard a lot. Some of it is confusing or even downright wrong:

- **Myth 1:** ADHD is just about being hyperactive.
- **Myth 2:** ADHD is an excuse for bad behavior.
- **Myth 3:** People with ADHD should try harder.
- **Myth 4:** ADHD is just an excuse for laziness.
- **Myth 5:** People with ADHD are just disorganized.

So, why do we need to break these myths? Because understanding leads to acceptance, and acceptance leads to progress. When you understand the challenges of ADHD, you'll start to see why housekeeping is like a battlefield. This doesn't mean making excuses or seeking special treatment; it means recognizing the real, significant challenges that people with ADHD face every day, including housekeeping.

ADHD Doesn't Mean Disorderly

Having ADHD doesn't mean you're disorderly. Not at all. It's not a flaw, not a failing, and definitely not a sign of chaos. Think of it more like a different operating system in a computer. It's not that it's disorganized; it just organizes things differently. People with ADHD are the thinkers, the dreamers, the explorers, and inventors in our society. Their minds are not limited by the conventional; they soar above it. Sure, you might struggle with focus and impulsivity, but who doesn't? We all have our quirks and challenges. What matters is how we handle them. ADHD can be managed with the right strategies, tools, and support. So, don't let the term "ADHD" make you feel disorderly. You're not—your brain works in a special way, and that's something to be celebrated, not stigmatized.

Embracing Unique Perspectives

Just like an explorer in a new land, you'll face challenges crossing unfamiliar terrains, but you also have the opportunity to discover new paths, hidden treasures, and breathtaking vistas that others might never see. That's what ADHD is like. It's a different journey, not a deficient one. Think about some of the world's most successful people. Many of them, like Richard Branson and Michael Phelps, have ADHD (Doyle, 2019; Dutton, 2007). They didn't get to where they are despite their ADHD; they got there because of it. Now, you might be thinking, *But what about the challenges?* and you're right—ADHD does come with its share of difficulties. But instead of seeing them as insurmountable hurdles, view them as something you can overcome with the right strategies and support. Just as every rose has its thorns, every person with ADHD has a unique blend of strengths and challenges. After all, isn't that what makes life interesting? The diversity, the different paths, the unique perspectives. It's time we embrace this in all its forms, including ADHD.

Shifting the Narrative

How do you embrace this mindset? By shifting the narrative. The way we perceive things has a profound impact on our behavior and attitudes. If we see ADHD as a crippling disorder, it becomes a self-fulfilling prophecy, making us feel inadequate and defeated. But if we reframe ADHD as a *unique* wiring of the brain that comes with its own strengths and advantages, it changes everything—our perception determines our reality. Imagine you've got this fantastic, high-powered sports car. It's shiny, it's loud, and it's super-fast. But there's a catch—it runs on a special kind of fuel, not the regular stuff. This doesn't make the car any less impressive or valuable, does it?

You hold the power to rewrite the story of your life, not as a spectator but as the main character. So, embrace the opportunity to shift your narrative, and just like that high-powered sports car, with the right fuel and care, you're unstoppable.

CASE STUDY: A DAY IN THE LIFE—ADHD AND THE BATTLE OF CLEANING

Noah, a 32-year-old self-employed video editor living alone, was diagnosed with ADHD in his early teens. Despite his high-functioning professional life, cleaning is one of Noah's biggest challenges. This case study illustrates the challenges he faces with cleaning and organization and shows how, with a little bit of self-compassion, there is a way to enhance his living conditions.

On a typical Saturday morning, Noah woke up with a plan: clean his apartment. He started in the living room, picking up a few scattered magazines, and spotted an interesting article on the cover. He promised himself a quick read, nothing more—30 minutes later, he was engrossed, the cleaning forgotten. After a while, he pulled away from the magazine, remembering what he needed to do. He shifted his focus to the kitchen, but as he picked up the dishes, he noticed leftovers from last night. He warmed them up, and as he waited, he opened up a YouTube tutorial on filmmaking. The leftovers got cold, the dishes stayed unwashed, and Noah was lost in the world of film editing. By the afternoon, Noah had tackled every cleaning task but completed none. He was frustrated, overwhelmed, and exhausted.

But Noah wasn't one to give up. He was always a positive guy, and he knew, deep down, he wasn't lazy or lacking discipline. It was his ADHD traits, the same ones that made him an exceptional problem-solver at work, tripping him up at home. Recognizing this, he'd gone from self-criticism to self-compassion. Then, he started with small tasks dedicated solely to picking up magazines, washing dishes, and so on. It wasn't perfect, but he was making progress. Yet, the struggle was real. Noah wished for a better way; a roadmap designed for minds like his. If only there were a way out for Noah and others fighting similar battles...

Key takeaway: In the grand scheme of things, understanding the landscape of ADHD and housekeeping is about harnessing your unique strengths and overcoming obstacles. ADHD's unique landscape might seem daunting at first, but it also offers a wealth of potential strategies *tailored* for you and Noah. Knowing why conventional cleaning methods don't work for you is the first step to devising ones that do.

2

ADHD-FRIENDLY CLEANING APPROACHES

Traditional cleaning methods, with their focus on meticulous organization and rigid schedules, miss the mark. They don't cater to the unique ADHD brain wiring that craves flexibility, spontaneity, and even a splash of fun. Aren't you tired of the maddening loop of clutter, procrastination, and guilt and ready to discover a cleaning approach *tailored* just for you?

WHY STANDARD METHODS FAIL

The truth is that traditional methods fail to deliver the cleanliness you desire because they aren't designed for you. As you know by now, the executive function of your brain, which plans, organizes, and executes tasks, works differently. Standard cleaning methods ask you to stick to a rigid routine or schedule and heavily rely on your ability to focus. These methods are too linear and mundane—incompatible with your wiring. The predictability is boring—that's why you lose focus. What you need are dynamic, engaging methods that work with your mind, not against it. Still not convinced?

Overwhelming Processes

Standard cleaning methods are like a complex symphony—so many overwhelming processes are involved. It's like trying to conduct a full orchestra when you can only listen to one instrument at a time. Conventional cleaning methods, like deep cleaning an entire house in one go, ask for long, uninterrupted periods of focus. When cleaning the kitchen, you'll be asked to scrub the countertops, clean out the refrigerator, mop the floor, and wash the dishes, among other things.

Each of these tasks requires a considerable amount of attention and time. For the average person, this is daunting enough, but for you—it's a dead end! Then there's the paradox of choice. Cleaning isn't a straightforward process, and there are different means to go about it, so there's no easy way to decide where to begin.

- Do you clean the bathroom first or the kitchen?
- Do you vacuum before you dust or after?

Decisions like these are paralyzing, making you give up before you even start. You might even struggle with perfectionism—if you can't do something perfectly, it's not worth doing at all. This mindset is particularly detrimental when it comes to cleaning.

Lack of Instant Gratification

Another reason your current methods fail is that your ADHD brain craves immediate rewards or gratification. It's not because you're incapable of understanding and valuing long-term benefits, but your brain's reward system is more tuned to immediate, tangible outcomes. Traditional cleaning techniques lack the instant gratification that keeps us motivated. It's like planting a seed and expecting a full-grown tree the next day. You scrubbed the sink, but the bathroom still looks dirty because the shower, toilet, and floor are yet to be cleaned. The effort doesn't feel rewarding or gratifying, so you lose interest and move on to something more immediate.

It's not that you're lazy or uninterested in cleanliness; it's simply that your brain doesn't get the instant reward it craves. Think, too, about the challenge of routine and repetition—two things the ADHD brain finds monotonous and unstimulating. Vacuuming, for example, involves repeating the same motion over and over again, often without a significant visible change. Your brain, hungry for stimulation and novelty, won't stick to it.

Misalignment With ADHD Strengths

Then there's the issue of methods that don't correspond to your ADHD strengths. Standard cleaning strategies are like a straight-jacket, rigid and suffocating, while you are like a free bird, thriving in flexibility and spontaneity. It's almost like asking a fish to climb a tree—it's not that the fish can't, but its natural abilities aren't suited to that. You're creative, you think outside the box, and you're a master of hyperfocus when a task truly interests you.

The problem is that standard cleaning methods don't utilize these unique strengths. They're systematic, methodical, repetitive—at odds with your ADHD mind:

- You clean room by room, starting from one corner and working your way around in a circle. But that's a linear process, which doesn't resonate with your nonlinear thinking.
- You declutter first and then deep clean, but this methodical approach doesn't cater to your strengths—spontaneity and versatility.

So, why do standard cleaning methods fail for you? Because they demand rigid routines and precise organization, not suitable for your vibrant, active mind. But you don't need to change—your approach does. When cleaning strategies resonate with your natural thought patterns, you're more likely to succeed.

TAILORING TO THE ADHD MIND

When you tailor cleaning methods to the ADHD mind, you create a *personalized strategy* that accommodates your strengths and weaknesses. What you get are *customized* cleaning methods just for you—methods that capitalize on your strengths. Just imagine how much you could accomplish if cleaning was less of a chore. Take a look at the difference and see which approaches sound more appealing:

Traditional cleaning will have you tackling large, unstructured tasks all at once:

- Setting aside a lot of time to clean the entire house. It's overwhelming; you'll procrastinate and leave things unfinished.
- Detailed cleaning plans, with specific tasks assigned to specific days, assume a level of consistency you might not have.

- Quiet, solo cleaning is monotonous and demands distraction.

ADHD-friendly cleaning breaks down tasks into manageable parts, providing clear direction and immediate results:

- Taking on one room or even part of a room at a time.
- Flexible plans that allow spontaneity. You might have a list of tasks each week, but the order and timing are up to you.
- Cleaning with background noise or company—listening to music, a podcast, or inviting a friend over.

Embrace the vibrant chaos of ADHD instead of trying to fit it into a conventional mold. The first step in doing this is to shift your focus to chunking tasks, a powerful strategy that regulates your active mind.

Chunking Tasks

Meet your new best friend: chunking tasks. Breaking tasks into smaller pieces is supported by the Attention Deficit Disorder Association (ADDA) (Team, 2022), which reports that it reduces the paralysis associated with ADHD:

- enhances focus
- boosts motivation
- improves time management
- reduces anxiety

Housekeeping is a broad term covering many things, so it's easy to get overwhelmed by it. But when you chunk it down to "tidy the bookshelf," "clean with windows," or "wash the sheets," it feels less intimidating and reduces ADHD symptoms (Sreenivas, 2022). Think of it as tackling a puzzle—instead of trying to visualize the whole picture at once, you focus on fitting together small sections one at a time. It's the same with chunking tasks:

1. **Identify the task:** Start by identifying the big things you need to do—those that you've been putting off or don't enjoy doing.
2. **Break it down:** Divide each task into several smaller tasks—make sure each small task is meaningful on its own and contributes to completing the larger task.
3. **Prioritize:** Arrange the smaller tasks based on their priority. The best way to do this is to decide based on time frame, urgency, or personal preference.

4. **Schedule:** Each task should be assigned a specific time slot. In this way, each task is given the attention it deserves.
5. **Take breaks:** Take your time; there's no rush. So, take short breaks to recharge and stay motivated between tasks.

Allocate time for each chore, and there you have it—a more manageable task list! But, while chunking tasks is all well and good, what if you could reward your brain with the satisfaction of visibly marked progress?

Visual Rewards

Think of visual rewards like a GPS guiding you through your goals—you're driving along a long, winding road, and you don't know where you're going. Suddenly, you see signposts along the way, pointing in the direction you need to go. That's what a visual reward does. It gives you a tangible sense of direction.

- Create a chart or a to-do list with checkboxes for every job you complete. Every time you tick off a task, it's like a little pat on the back, a mini celebration.

But it's not just about ticking boxes. Visual rewards take many forms:

- **Time-lapse video:** Set your phone up in a spot with a full view and press record. After you're done cleaning, stop the recording. Watching the transformation unfold in fast-forward will give you a clear, satisfying view of your hard work.
- **Color-coded cleaning supplies:** Colors stimulate the brain—the right one can improve focus (green, orange, blue), manage stress (muted yellow, green), and boost cognitive functioning (warm colors) (Koltuska-Haskin, 2023). Assign different color labels to different tasks, like blue for the duster, yellow for the anti-bac spray, and so on.
- **Progress bar or thermometer:** For every job you do, score yourself 5 points. Then, for every time you hit 20, do something nice for yourself.
- **Token jar:** Use an old mason jar or a transparent container and give yourself $5 for every task you complete. Once you've filled the jar, reward yourself with a treat or a break.

Visual rewards work because they tap into our natural desire for achievement and reward. No matter what kind of visual reward system you use, the key is to make it tangible and visible. This way, you're working toward an abstract goal, as well as something you can see, touch, and feel.

With a few cleaning strategies under your belt, you're ready to take the next step. Now it's time to channel the power of hyper-focus so you'll meet and then exceed your cleaning goals.

Leveraging Hyperfocus

Cleaning involves many steps and details, and hyper-focus lets you zone in on these with an intensity that others can't match. Think about it:

- When you're hyper-focused on cleaning your kitchen, you won't just wash the dishes and wipe the countertops; you'll notice the crumbs in the corners of your drawers, the grease splatters behind the stove, and the dust under the refrigerator.
- With hyperfocus, you might not simply hang up clothes and call it a day. Instead, you'll sort them by color, season, or type of clothing, making it easy to find what you need.

You'll have to learn how to manage it, though, so you can clean and organize without letting it consume your entire day:

- **Use a timer:** Set a timer for 15 or 30 minutes to help you focus on one job at a time.
- **Break it down:** Channel your hyper-focus on completing one task at a time.
- **Use our checklist (found at the end of this book):** Stay organized with a clear sequence of tasks so you don't miss anything.
- **Use visual prompts:** Post notes around your home to jog your memory and keep you on track.

Tailor cleaning methods to your ADHD mind, and you're acknowledging and respecting your unique way of interacting with the world. Remember, there's no right or wrong way to clean—only what works best for you. But crafting a cleaning strategy that suits your ADHD traits isn't just about decluttering and organizing; it's also about setting yourself up for continuous success.

SETTING UP FOR SUCCESS

Preparing for success is just as important as the cleaning itself—you're creating an environment where ADHD doesn't hold the reins. To do this means to take control and build an environment conducive for success based on your *unique* ADHD brain.

The Right Tools

Cleaning is easier and more effective when you use the right equipment. Each tool in your arsenal should make you feel good, or at least not dread using them.

- **Scented all-purpose cleaner and disinfecting wipes:** Go for cleaners with your favorite scents—the fresh smell of citrus, the calming scent of lavender, or the invigorating aroma of eucalyptus.
- **Microfiber cloths:** These little beauties are an absolute gem. They're incredibly absorbent but also soft to the touch—such a pleasure to use as they glide smoothly over surfaces.
- **Colorful cleaning tools**: Choose tools in your favorite color or pattern—an incredible motivator to use them. Think cool-looking mops, vibrant scrub brushes, or patterned dustpan and brush.

- **Ergonomic design:** Ergonomic tools provide a better grip, reducing the strain on your hands and making cleaning less physically taxing. Look for vacuum cleaners, a mop, and a bucket with this kind of design—make sure they're colorful too!
- **Weighted cleaning tools:** Just like a weighted blanket, weighted cleaning tools are calming. They'll improve your control while cleaning, too, because you'll be able to feel the tool.
- **Textured gloves:** If you don't like the feel of certain surfaces or cleaners, look for gloves that are nice on the skin. They'll protect your hands and feel good as you wear them—double win!

Now that you have the right cleaning tools in hand, there's something else to fast-track your ADHD-friendly cleaning—environmental cues.

Environmental Cues

Your surroundings shape your habits and actions, so strategically arranging and designing your space will naturally encourage and support your cleaning routine. Environmental cues are elements or triggers in our surroundings that prompt us to take action. Think of them as gentle reminders or nudges that prod you into doing what needs to be done, thus bypassing the need for internal motivation or remembering to do the task.

How can you use environmental cues effectively for a successful cleaning strategy?

- Choose obvious and meaningful—a brightly colored cleaning caddy in a conspicuous spot in each room. Then, every time you walk into the room, the sight of the caddy will prompt you to spend a few minutes tidying up.
- Use labels and designated places for your supplies. Labels make cleanup faster and easier by giving you visual cues of where things belong.
- Post-it notes are a classic. Stick them around your home—on the fridge, bathroom mirror, or computer screen to remind you what needs to be done.
- Use temptation bundling and pair a task you're not so enthusiastic about (like vacuuming) with an activity you love—perhaps listening to your favorite artist or funny podcast.
- Use a whiteboard or a chalkboard to track your progress—the satisfaction of crossing off completed tasks is very motivating.

No matter how you set up your environment to support your efforts, remember that the goal is to maintain cleanliness and order with less effort. Simple yet powerful, environmental cues work subtly, tapping into your visual and kinesthetic learning style and making the process of cleaning almost automatic. Want to know what happens when you pair these cues with positive reinforcement?

Positive Reinforcement

Positive reinforcement is a principle of behavioral psychology—like giving a high-five to your brain when you do something right. Essentially, it's the process of encouraging and rewarding good behavior to increase the likelihood of you repeating said behavior (Valmiki et al., 2021). For it to work for you means recognizing the good and making a big deal about it. Imagine you're training a puppy. Every time the puppy does something you want— like sitting on command or not chewing the furniture, you reward it with a treat or a cuddle. The puppy enjoys this, so it repeats that behavior in hopes of getting more rewards. That's positive reinforcement in action.

ADHD brains are wired a bit differently. They have a deficit in dopamine, a neurotransmitter responsible for motivation and reward (Blum et al., 2008). This deficit makes it difficult for you to feel motivated, stay on task, or complete things that aren't immediately rewarding. Positive reinforcement fills this dopamine deficit. When you reward yourself for doing a good job, your brain releases dopamine. This not only feels great, but it also motivates you to repeat the behavior in the future. It doesn't have to be anything big; small rewards work, too:

- Indulging in your favorite snack after dusting the blinds.
- Watching an episode of your latest Netflix obsession after every 30 minutes of cleaning.
- Going for a walk (a powerful antidote to stress, anxiety, and depression) once you've tackled the mess in your bedroom.

After treating yourself to that well-deserved reward for a cleaning job well done, here's a story of how one cleaning mishap, with a little resilience and a positive outlook, morphed into a victory.

A FAILED CLEANING EXPERIMENT TURNED SUCCESS

Vivacious, innovative, and intelligent, Jamal lived in the heart of Chicago. Jamal had ADHD, so cleaning and organizing was a monumental task. His house was a world of its own—kitchen sink hidden beneath unwashed utensils, laundry bins overflowing, and a living room floor he couldn't walk on without having to dodge something. Every attempt at making order out of chaos seemed to, ironically, bring more chaos.

One day, Jamal decided to embark on a cleaning spree. Armed with determination and a Pinterest list of cleaning hacks, he plunged into the whirlpool of disorder. The result? The same as always—forgetfulness and distractibility turned hours into days, days into weeks, and Jamal's house was still a mess. Feeling defeated, he did what he always did—endlessly scrolling through TikTok to escape his bad feelings. He came across a TikTok video suggesting ADHD-specific cleaning strategies. Jamal started by tackling one thing at a time —keeping common areas clean, putting things away where they were used, and making cleaning supplies accessible in every room. He ran the dishwasher every night, even if it wasn't completely full, and started using timers and reminders for laundry. The turning point came when he discovered "temptation bundling." He started watching his favorite shows only when folding laundry! This trick magically turned a boring task into something fun and achievable.

Jamal's failed cleaning experiment had turned into a success. He learned that ADHD-friendly cleaning approaches were not about perfection but about finding a routine that worked for him. His story is a testament to the fact that cleaning isn't a project but a daily habit born from ADHD traits—a lesson we can all learn from.

Key takeaway: Standard cleaning methods don't work because they're not suited to your ADHD brain. Now you're armed with the right mindset and tools, and you're ready for the next exciting shift—identifying the zones of importance around your home so you can put your techniques to good use.

3

ZONES OF IMPACT

Imagine your home as a lush, vibrant garden full of potential and beauty. Every individual flower bed needs your special attention. With ADHD, it can seem like you're trying to tend to every plant, weed, and patch of soil all at once—it's not feasible. Instead, think of the key areas in your home—the kitchen, the living room, the bedroom, as your "zones of importance." They're like the sunflowers, roses, and lilies in your garden—the spots drawing your attention first and need your care the most. Like a thoughtful gardener, you make sure they're well-watered, pruned, and pest-free before moving on to the next plant. In your home, it makes sense to clean and organize these key areas first—after doing so, you'll find it much easier to manage the rest of your "garden" (home). It's not about trying to do it all at once but rather understanding where to plant your attention first.

IDENTIFYING ZONES

Put on your Sherlock Holmes hat because you're on a mission to find the dirt and grime taking refuge in your home's most secret corners. With your new detective's eye, it's time to identify zones around the home.

- The first place to start is the high-traffic areas—places like your living room, kitchen, and hallways, where you and your family spend the most time. These areas are usually the dirtiest simply because they see the most use.
- Next, let's move to your personal spaces—your bedroom, bathroom, and home office, where you spend your private time. These areas might not seem as dirty as the high-traffic areas, but they accumulate dust and grime, nonetheless.
- Let's not forget those neglected corners. The areas we usually overlook—behind furniture, under the bed, or the top of the fridge.

Let's start with pinpointing those high-traffic areas, and you'll be well on your way toward a new and focused cleaning strategy.

High Traffic Areas

You know the feeling. You've just finished a marathon cleaning session, and your home is sparkling. But within a few days... chaos! It's like a tornado swept through, tossing things haphazardly, and you're back to square one. If you've found yourself in this never-ending cycle, it's time to identify the high-traffic areas in your home. These are the spots in your home that see the most footfall. Think of your kitchen, living room, hallways, or even your bathroom. The wear and tear in these areas are much more noticeable because, well, they're popular! Everyone in the house uses them, and often too.

By targeting high-traffic areas, you're addressing the mess where it happens most. Take a look around your home. Where does everyone seem to congregate? If living alone, where do you spend the most time? Where do the majority of messes occur? Think of areas like:

- kitchen
- living room
- bathroom
- office
- entrance/hallway

Keeping these high-traffic areas clean and organized will improve your home's overall appearance and functionality, making your quality of life that much better. Remember, though, to pace yourself, you don't need to do everything all at once. Make a list and tackle one area at a time.

Or you can do everything at once.

The beauty of ADHD-friendly cleaning techniques is you get to decide how things get done. What makes a difference is that you now have methods specifically *tailored* to you.

Personal Spaces

Personal spaces are your zones of control. They're areas you alone manage and maintain according to your own preferences and habits. When you define your own space, you take charge of it. You have the freedom to decide what goes in and what stays out. Tidying up then becomes less like a tedious chore and more like empowerment.

Identifying personal spaces creates a sense of responsibility. When a space is yours, you're more likely to take care of it. It's like having your own little garden—you water it, tend to it, and you don't let the weeds take over. Plus, personal spaces reduce conflicts, especially if you live with others, because everyone has their own ideas about what's clean and what's cluttered. By having designated personal spaces, you avoid stepping on each other's toes—you organize your space your way, and they can do the same with theirs.

There's also something comforting and secure about having your own personal space. Here, you can retreat, relax, and just be yourself. When that space is clean and organized, you're not only at peace, but you're more focused and less overstimulated (Aliouche, 2022). So, if you're finding it hard to stay on top of cleaning and organizing, take a moment to identify your personal spaces in your home:

- bedroom
- office
- backyard
- garage
- living room
- spare room

Now, onto identifying the unseen areas—those that subtly impact your home just as much as your personal areas.

The Often-Neglected Corners

The nooks and crannies of our home are so often overlooked because they're usually the places that are out of sight, out of mind. Think about the top shelf in your closet, the space behind your fridge, or the corner of your garage. You don't see these areas every day, so it's easy to forget they exist. But just because you can't see the dust and clutter doesn't mean it's not there:

- behind appliances, think fridges, ovens, and washing machines
- under furniture, like beds, sofas, and tables
- inside cupboards and drawers
- light fixtures and ceiling fans
- window sills and frames
- behind toilets
- under rugs and carpets
- air vents and ducts
- garbage and recycling bins
- behind doors
- baseboards and crown moldings
- inside the oven and microwave
- the tops of cabinets and wardrobes
- patio and outdoor furniture
- computer keyboards and remote controls

Dust and clutter have a sneaky way of spreading, so if you clean these areas regularly, you'll find that the rest of your home stays cleaner and more organized as well.

Just like a winning game plan hinges on understanding your high-impact zones, knowing your home's cleaning hotspots is half the battle won. Now that you've got the map, it's time to chart your course—deciding which areas demand immediate attention and which can wait.

PRIORITIZING EFFORTS

Prioritizing your cleaning tasks means identifying specific areas in your home that need attention and systematically dealing with them. The advantage of this approach is that it allows you to focus your energy and time on one zone at a time, which reduces the pressure that comes with large cleaning projects. For the ADHD brain, this method is particularly beneficial—it aligns with your unique thought patterns and helps manage your mental energy better. It all starts with small steps to inspire big changes.

Quick Wins

Quick wins are tasks you initiate, accomplish, and cross off quickly. You'll see visible results in a short time, so you get immediate gratification. To get quick wins from cleaning your home, start by identifying small tasks that instantly enhance the appearance of your environment:

- a quick wipe of your window sills or the kitchen countertops
- make your bed first thing in the morning
- make the rubbish out
- tidy up the coffee table or dining table
- disinfect doorknobs, light switches, and remote controls

These jobs may seem small, but they'll add up as you tackle them one by one. Trying to do too much at once will be overwhelming and counterproductive. By focusing on one quick win at a time, you'll gradually tidy up your home without feeling the burden.

As you experience these quick wins, you'll discover a tidy space isn't just visually pleasing—it's emotionally liberating, too! How would it feel if you alone could boost your productivity, reduce your anxiety, and lift your spirits?

Emotional Impacts of Clean Spaces

Imagine walking into your living room full of serenity and order—the soft scent of fresh linen, the sight of neatly arranged books on the shelf, and the feel of a polished table. There's a distinct sense of calm and control around this because a clean space is a visual and sensory representation of order and predictability. This feeling is amplified in the ADHD brain—a clutter-free environment is a soothing balm to your often chaotic thought patterns, reducing distractions and promoting focus and productivity.

- Take, for instance, the simple act of retrieving a spoon from a tidy drawer. There's no need to rummage through a mismatch of cutlery or get sidetracked by other items. That simple, clean order dissolves stress and is a testament to your capability and self-sufficiency.
- After deep cleaning your bathroom, the mirror shines brightly, the tiles glisten, and the air smells fresh. As you run a warm bath, the cleanliness of the space amplifies your relaxation.

A clean space is more than just visual tidiness. It's a sensory experience evoking calm, control, and success. So, take advantage of this feeling whenever you can; you'll soon come to love that feeling and do all you can to maintain it. As you indulge in this empowering effect, you'll find yourself naturally drawn toward progressive cleaning strategies—a systematic approach to maintaining your haven of calm.

Progressive Cleaning

Cleaning doesn't have to be an all-or-nothing effort. To clean progressively means you're breaking down overwhelming chores into smaller, simpler steps:

1. You start by tidying up a single drawer.
2. Then, move on to the entire cabinet.
3. Until eventually, your whole room sparkles.

The beauty of progressive cleaning is that it works with the ADHD brain's need for instant gratification. You gain pride in every small task you complete, encouraging you to keep going. The point is to set a pace that works for you so you can maintain order without feeling stressed. It's a great way to take control of your environment. And the best part? It's completely achievable!

- Start with 5 minutes of cleaning each day, gradually increasing the time as you become comfortable. Feel free to use timers or alarms to keep track.

It may sound trivial to start so small, but over time, you'll notice the difference—not just in your surroundings but in your overall well-being. How? As you embrace the benefits of progressive cleaning, you find it naturally leading you toward a structured strategy—a routine where the areas in your home receive regular attention.

ROTATION CLEANING SYSTEM

ADHD often impairs executive functioning skills, which makes it difficult to initiate and accomplish tasks (Villines, 2023). A rotational cleaning system is an innovative approach to deal with this. It'll leverage your executive function, the brain's command center, to organize cleaning so it's easier to start, follow through, and complete. Not only will you find this approach makes cleaning less intimidating, but you'll also notice it improves your mood and motivation (Gawrilow et al., 2011). Now, how's that for a win-win cleaning solution?

Mapping the Zones

The first thing you'll need to do is map the zones of your home:

- Imagine your home as a city and each room is a different neighborhood.
- Each neighborhood has its own unique characteristics and needs.

This strategy borrows from the 5S system, a Japanese efficiency methodology designed to reduce waste and increase productivity.

Step 1: Identify your zones:

Let's note down the areas of your home based on the zones we identified earlier:

- **Zone 1:** High-traffic areas—living room and kitchen.
- **Zone 2:** Personal spaces—bedroom and home office.
- **Zone 3:** Those neglected corners—behind appliances or inside cupboards.

Step 2: Sketch your zones:

Now, symbolizing each zone on a timeline to create a visual map. Grab a pen and paper and roughly draw an outline of your home. Then, color code each zone in terms of priority. This doesn't need to be perfect; you just need a visual representation of these zones.

1. **Zone 1:** Red (high priority)
2. **Zone 2:** Blue (mid-priority)
3. **Zone 3:** Yellow (low priority)

This example is just that—an example. By all means, customize this system to suit *you*. The beauty of an ADHD-specific cleaning system is its flexibility. You can *tailor* it to match your ADHD traits and the features of your home. Feel free to conduct your home cleaning in a way that resonates with you!

Setting a Timetable

With a cleaning timetable, you're setting up a framework to guide you through the maze of time management and organization. It's a powerful tool to help manage your ADHD. Here's why:

- **Provides structure:** By avoiding the paralysis that comes from not knowing where to start, a timetable shows you what needs to be done and when.
- **Manage overwhelm:** Instead of looking at a whole house that needs to be cleaned, you're just focusing on one task at a time.
- **Develop and maintain a routine:** Stick to a timetable and you'll soon have a routine. A routine provides stability and control, reducing anxiety and improving focus (Bettino, 2021).

Now, you don't have to have anything too rigid—unless, of course, that's what you want!

1. Start by listing the cleaning zones in terms of priority.
2. Then, break these areas into manageable chunks—maybe you clean the toilet and sink on Monday, the bath/shower on Tuesday, mop the floor on Wednesday, and so on.
3. Next, allocate specific time slots for these tasks. It could be the first thing in the morning, right after work, or whenever you feel most energetic.

Remember, this timetable is not set in stone. Adjust as needed if certain tasks are too overwhelming or certain times aren't working. Start however you need, even if it's just folding the laundry on day one. After a while, you'll become more comfortable with the routine and can gradually add more tasks to your day, even week. The main thing is to be consistent and patient with yourself—Rome wasn't built in a day, and neither will your cleaning routine be perfect on the first try. If you want to encourage consistency and success the first time, don't forget the checklist at the end of the book. If you want to encourage success the first time, don't forget the checklist at the end of the book. In the meantime, keep reading to keep things consistent.

Ensuring Consistency

Cleaning, with its repetitive nature and lack of immediate rewards, is hard enough as it is. With ADHD, it's easy to become overwhelmed, lose focus, or forget what you're supposed to be doing. But this doesn't mean you're doomed to a life of chaos—with the right strategies, you can stick to a cleaning schedule, just like anyone else. Here's how:

- **Visualize your success:** Literally, picture yourself following your routine seamlessly. It's like a mental rehearsal—the more you imagine it, the more you'll make it a reality.
- **Break it down:** Chunking can't be emphasized enough. Large tasks are the antithesis of motivation and focus.
- **Be flexible:** Allow some wiggle room in your schedule. Life happens, and sometimes things don't go as planned, so don't beat yourself up over minor deviations.
- **Find your "why":** Recognizing *why* you want to stick to a routine is a major motivation booster. Is it to achieve a specific goal? Do you have a party coming up? Or maybe you want to beat the mess altogether? Whatever the "why," keep it in mind and let it fuel your dedication.

- **Make it fun:** It sounds cliché, but it works wonders. We're naturally inclined to do things we enjoy, and when things are fun to do, we become more engaged with them.

Ensuring consistency is never as easy as it sounds—life happens, and juggling multiple responsibilities makes cleanings the last thing you want to deal with. But here's the thing: Cleaning doesn't have to be stressful or time-consuming. Yes, it's easier said than done, but even small, achievable goals make all the difference.

FINDING PEACE BY ADDRESSING JUST ONE ZONE

For Jenny, a picture-perfect home was a distant dream. Sharing the responsibility of the care of their elderly mother with her siblings—they had each other over dinner every weekend. When it was Jenny's turn to host the much-anticipated weekend meal, she panicked. The dining room was nothing short of an obstacle course —"I had no choice but to get stuck in," she said. Taking a deep breath, she rolled up her sleeves and dived into the challenge. The cluttered table, disordered shelves, messy floor, and dusty corners gradually transformed under her determination. Each swipe of the duster and reorganized item was like a therapeutic release, and soon enough, the room slowly resembled her internal journey—from panic to calm, from disorder to harmony. As the last of the clutter was in its place, Jenny felt a wave of tranquility wash over her—"for the first time in a long time, I felt in control."

The dinner came and went ("lamb and veg"). As Jenny cleared the table, she realized that peace wasn't such a distant dream after all—"cleaning my dining room was more than just cleaning; it was a step toward bringing peace into my home. I swore from now on, I'd tackle each room one day at a time."

Key takeaway: Just like Jenny, you have the power to transform your life one zone at a time. Prioritize your efforts with a rotation cleaning system, and you'll build a habit of organization and discipline. Now we've got our zones set up; how about we spice things up a bit and make cleaning not just productive but genuinely fun?

4

MAKING CLEANING FUN AND REWARDING

Play is our brain's favorite way of learning.

— DIANE ACKERMAN

Ackerman was right, and it isn't just a cute saying; it's scientifically grounded! Play fuels our brain's natural learning processes by stimulating the brain's development and function (Wang & Aamodt, 2012). It boosts creativity, encourages problem-solving, and builds resilience. What's more, the human brain is naturally inclined toward playful activities. This makes play an effective learning tool, even for adults. So, how can you incorporate play into mundane chores and transform them into rewarding experiences?

GAMIFYING CLEANING

Cleaning made fun turns dreary household tasks into less of a drag. Think of it as turning your house into an adventure land where ironing or vacuuming earns you points or propels you to the next level. And the best part is you're the game master, setting your own rules and rewards.

Setting Rewards

Think about the last time you completed a task that felt impossible. Imagine if, after all that effort, you treat yourself to a nice reward. It's not silly, it's smart. Why? Because it instills a sense of motivation and self-appreciation. Our brains love rewards. It's a simple psychological trick, turning a mundane task into an exciting challenge. You're giving yourself a pat on your own back, a way of acknowledging your efforts and saying, "Well done." The idea is to reward yourself with something relaxing and enjoyable:

- Book a day at the spa to relax and rejuvenate. As an alternative, make your own spa

experience at home with a warm bath, essential oils, and soothing music.
- Watch that film or series you've been wanting to see and cozy up with popcorn and blankets for the ultimate home cinema experience.
- Buy a new piece of decor for your home, like a painting, a plant, or a decorative cushion.
- Plan a day for outdoor activities like hiking, cycling, or a picnic in the park.
- Enjoy an uninterrupted hour or two reading that book you've been meaning to get to.
- Take some time to indulge in your favorite hobby.
- Invest in a new plant for your garden or indoor collection.
- Take a trip to your local coffee shop and enjoy your favorite brew or try something new.

No matter if you're rewarding yourself with a slice of cake, a new book, or an episode of your favorite show, try to resist the temptation to indulge yourself until after the job is done. Patience is key! Don't shortchange your efforts by dipping into that reward early—stick to your guns, complete the task, relish the accomplishment, and then indulge yourself.

ADHD-Friendly Challenges

With ADHD-friendly cleaning challenges, the path to your rewards becomes more exciting and achievable, enhancing your inherent competitiveness and boosting motivation. They build resilience and unlock untapped potential by pushing the boundaries of comfort. The beauty lies not just in achieving the goal but in the transformation it initiates.

- **Beat the clock:** Set a timer for 15 minutes and see how much you can clean before time runs out. Cleaning becomes a race against time, getting your adrenaline pumping. It also helps to maintain focus since it motivates you to complete as much cleaning as possible within the given timeframe.
- **Theme day cleaning:** Assign every day of the week a specific cleaning task, like "Washing Wednesday" or "Tidy-up Tuesday." Cleaning this way adds a fun twist to your chores and helps you organize your zones. It also provides a sense of routine and predictability.
- **Dance and clean:** Dancing reduces stress and increases endorphins (Edwards, 2017)—blast your favorite upbeat music and get moving. Cleaning this way is not only enjoyable but also a great way to express yourself and let loose.

Setting and following through on any of these challenges is a testament to your adaptability and evolution. So, try them whenever you can—even if you feel silly. Think of them as a process of metamorphosis, through which weaknesses become strengths.

As you take on these challenges, remember to pause and acknowledge your progress, no matter how small. Because for a calmer home and mind, it's these small victories that reinforce your self-worth and encourage a positive mindset.

Celebrating Small Victories

Okay, so you've spent 20 minutes decluttering the hallway. It might not seem like a big deal in light of all the other jobs waiting for you, but it's worth celebrating. These tiny triumphs *are* achievements—never forget that. As you go, you're continually progressing toward a cleaner, more organized home, and every step counts!

- Create a checklist—here's something immensely satisfying about ticking off a task once it's done. For example, you've just finished scrubbing the bathtub till it shines—tick. You've dusted and polished your desk—tick. Each tick is a small victory.
- Don't shy away from taking before and after photos. It might seem silly at first, but these will

show the hard work you've put into everything so far and are tangible proof of your efforts.

In the grand scheme of things, celebrating after cleaning out the sock drawer might seem trivial, but remember, the space we live in directly impacts our mental well-being. When your home is clean, clutter-free, and peaceful, positivity and productivity thrive.

Now, it's time to elevate the cleaning experience even more.

THE POWER OF MUSIC AND PODCASTS

Every time you press "play" on your favorite music or podcast, you're tapping into a power that's both profound and scientifically supported. Picture this: As you scrub the floors or dust the shelves, the rhythm of your chosen soundtrack syncs with your actions, creating a therapeutic, almost meditative state. Podcasts, on the other hand, turn cleaning into a learning experience. As you vacuum and declutter, you absorb new ideas and stories, stimulating your creativity and encouraging empathy. Let's take a look.

Creating Cleaning Playlists

Music stimulates the release of dopamine, the "feel-good" neurotransmitter, which makes tedious chores like cleaning a lot more fun (McGilchrist, 2011). It's not just about the beat and tempo, either. The lyrics, melody, and even memories tied to a particular song boost your mood and motivation (Fabiny, 2015). The trick is to choose songs that keep your energy up, stimulating your brain enough to keep you focused but not so much that you get distracted.

- Start by picking songs you love. This is your playlist, after all, so it should include music that makes you happy. Think of high-energy tunes that make you want to move—whether it's pop, rock, hip-hop, or EDM, it doesn't matter as long as it makes you feel good.
- For those times when you're anxious and just want to focus and maintain energy, create a playlist of ADHD-specific music (Lo-fi, Isochronic, Solfeggio, Binaural). Their steady rhythm and soothing tones work by aligning your brainwaves with the beats, promoting concentration, motivation, and emotional balance.

While music has many benefits, consider switching things up now and again with an engaging podcast—a perfect way to transform your routine into a mentally stimulating experience.

Engaging the Mind

Just think how time will fly when cleaning out your drawers, engrossed in a riveting discussion about black holes in a far-off galaxy, or laughing out loud to a hilarious Chris Rock anecdote while folding laundry. That's the power of podcasts. Unlike visual mediums, they rely on your imagination and active listening skills. And multitasking is easier with them. When your hands are busy, your mind is free to focus on absorbing new information or getting lost in an engaging narrative. It's like fueling your brain with intriguing content while your body stays productive.

There are over 5 million podcasts on Spotify, so you'll have plenty to choose from (Cridland, 2022). Some of the most popular topics are:

- advice
- true-crime
- quirky facts
- random knowledge
- comedy
- celebrity news
- book and movie reviews

Isn't it incredible how a good podcast can turn a routine activity into a learning opportunity? Now, imagine pairing that with a rhythmic backdrop—the steady beat elevating your chores into a lively dance.

The Joy of Rhythm

Rhythm is like the heartbeat of life, pulsing through music, the seasons, and even our daily routines. It's a universal language our bodies naturally respond to. Have you ever noticed how you instinctively tap your foot to a catchy tune? That's your body syncing with the rhythm and subtly affecting focus and attention.

Now, let's bring rhythm into cleaning. By setting a rhythmic pace to your cleaning tasks—say, sweeping the floor or moving around to the beat of your favorite song, you create a flow that keeps you engaged with the job. This rhythmic engagement improves cognitive functions like short-term memory, concentration, and visual perception (Zanto et al., 2022). But it's not just about focus. Rhythm also has a profound effect on our moods. Rhythmic activities, like dancing or drumming, induce a state of "flow," a deep, immersive state of concentration that boosts happiness and reduces stress (Chirico et al., 2015)

Now, think about combining that rhythm-induced flow with the camaraderie of friends. Group cleaning can take rhythm-filled cleanups to a whole new level, turning a solitary chore into a social activity.

GROUP CLEANING

If you struggle to focus for long periods of time while cleaning solo, then group cleaning is for you—instead of facing the mess alone, you and your friends or family members tackle it together. Just imagine the laughter, camaraderie, and shared satisfaction as your group transforms chaos into order. It's not just about getting things done faster; group cleaning fosters teamwork, builds relationships, and creates a sense of shared responsibility. Plus, it's a whole lot less daunting by lightening the load. In the end, teamwork makes the dream work. We achieve our goals faster and cultivate a sense of community when we pool our resources, skills, and energy.

Collaborative Efforts

Think back to the times when you've hosted a get-together at your home. The music's great, the food's delicious, and the company's delightful. But when the last guest leaves, you're left with a mess that seems impossible to deal with alone. Now, picture the same scenario, but this time, your friends pitch in to help with the cleanup. Besides being manageable, it's fun as well. That's the power of collaborative cleaning. It harnesses the strength of teamwork and shared responsibility, where each of you arm yourselves with a different cleaning tool, moving around the house in a choreographed dance of sorts. Suddenly, everything is less intimidating. It's like a game of tag where the "it" is the dirt and you're on a mission to tag it out. Plus, there are many ways you can make collaborative cleaning fun:

- Make a list of everything you need to do. Bring it to life with colorful markers and stickers (with the zones of importance in mind). The rule of the game is simple—pick a task, complete it, and get the satisfaction of striking it off the list.
- Don't shy away from friendly competition by seeing who can finish their task faster or better. Stick to a weekly timetable and switch roles every week to keep things interesting.
- Turn the cleaning spree into an event by playing some upbeat music with some food or drink to keep you energized. Sing along, dance, and let the rhythm guide your cleaning moves. Before you know it, you're not just cleaning; you're creating memories and bonding with the people you love.

Let's not forget the satisfying sight of a squeaky-clean home at the end of the day. Getting to this point proves that when you work together, even the dullest tasks are an exciting group activity. To really get things going, though, you're going to need some rewards!

Social Rewards

It's all well and good roping your friend or family into your cleaning, but there will undoubtedly come a time when things become a tad unmotivating—someone gets too engrossed in scrolling, or you get distracted by what's inside an old box of forgotten treasures. Maybe even the day's been long and tiring. You feel like giving up but then someone acknowledges your efforts, saying, "You've done an amazing job organizing those files!" That simple act of recognition is a social reward. And it's incredibly important in group cleaning situations, or any group task for that matter.

Social rewards are non-tangible recognitions that boost morale and enhance motivation—just as much as money and food do (Bhanji & Delgado, 2013). They're based on ability-centered or effort-centered success, implicitly stating, "I see you, I value your contribution, and your hard work hasn't gone unnoticed." When things start to dwindle, use them to keep things positive, increase job satisfaction, and make people feel appreciated. In turn, you'll discover just how inspired you are to keep pushing, even when the job feels impossible.

Social rewards don't cost a thing but make a world of difference. And offering social rewards is easier than you think:

- "Well done with the kitchen! Your cleaning skills are top-notch. How about we celebrate with a pizza night next time?"
- "You've outdone yourself with the bathroom. You've earned yourself an extra hour of TV time tonight." (for the kids)
- "Wow, you've made the garage spotless! That calls for a date night, your pick!"

Just as social rewards motivate and uplift spirits, accountability partners push us to achieve more than we ever thought possible. Both utilize the power of community and human connection to fuel performance and productivity.

Accountability Partners

An accountability partner is someone who holds you responsible for your actions and decisions, especially when you're working toward a goal. They're like your personal cheerleader, but one who isn't afraid to give you a bit of tough love when you need it. Think of your close friends or family members—they know you well and can support you personally. Even local community groups or cleaning clubs can be a place to share similar goals and exchange strategies. While group cleaning, an accountability partner

- checks to make sure you're staying on task.
- encourages you when you're feeling unmotivated.
- joins you in celebrating when that seemingly insurmountable pile of clutter disappears.
- gives you a gentle nudge when you're drifting off.
- reflects your progress, reminding you how far you've come.

This accountability is particularly important if you have ADHD. Having someone to answer to gives you structure and a sense of purpose, which helps you get things done.

In the grand scheme of things, accountability partners are key in transforming daunting tasks into achievable goals. They bring out the best in you, keep you grounded, and remind you of your capabilities. So, when the going gets tough, remember, you don't have to go it alone.

TURNING A DREADED CLEANING DAY INTO A PARTY

Meet Hana, a 28-year-old call handler diagnosed with ADHD in her early twenties. Cleaning her apartment was one of her dreaded tasks because it called for focus and organization. It was a tornado of clothes, books, and pizza boxes, enough to make anyone's heart sink. But Hana decided to turn things around by transforming the drudgery into a delightful cleaning party.

"Music, munchies, and mops," Hana declared with a twinkle in her eye. To distract herself from the mundane chores, she knew the trick was to make them exciting. As the beats of her favorite songs filled the room, her energy levels skyrocketed. With every beat, she twirled and dusted, danced, and decluttered; her mop was her dance partner, and the broom her backup dancer. While scrubbing dishes in rhythm with the music, she used her imagination to make the monotonous task of washing dishes feel like she was playing a water drum. Midway through, she had a pizza break. Munching on her favorite pepperoni pizza, she looked around her half-clean apartment and was pleased with herself—she was actually having fun!

Hana's story reminds us that sometimes, the key to accomplishing difficult jobs is to change the way we look at them.

Key takeaway: Cleaning doesn't have to be boring. Make it fun and see the extraordinary potential of these ADHD cleaning hacks. While having fun is great for motivation, recognizing any emotional blocks will significantly boost your progress.

5

OVERCOMING EMOTIONAL BARRIERS

In the previous chapter, our focus was predominantly on the tactical aspects of housekeeping with ADHD. We looked at the nuts and bolts, understanding how you can utilize your unique traits to build a cleaning strategy *right for you*. As we transition into the forthcoming chapters, we'll shift our focus from the tactical to the strategic. We're moving from the "why" to the "how," from the mindset to the tools.

As we know by now, ADHD impacts more than just attention and impulsivity. It's a significant player in our executive function, which coordinates our thoughts, actions, and ability to plan. But here's something even more intriguing: Around 70% of individuals with ADHD also struggle with emotional regulation (Lovering, 2022). If cleaning and organizing your home makes you feel bad, then it's possible these are emotional barriers preventing you from getting started or finishing in a way you're happy with.

IDENTIFYING BLOCKS

Take a look around. Does the mess and clutter make you feel overwhelmed, frustrated, or even embarrassed? Do these feelings then prevent you from getting into the thick of it? To overcome these barriers means to look at why they're there in the first place—are you worried about doing it perfectly? Or are you scared of throwing something important away? By recognizing these emotional hurdles, you can learn to address them head-on.

Fear of Starting

Have you ever heard the saying, "A journey of a thousand miles begins with a single step?" For many of us, especially those dealing with ADHD, the first step is the hardest to take— being paralyzed by a cluttered room and not knowing where to start. It's like trying to solve a jigsaw puzzle with thousands of pieces—you're excited at first, but as you look at the pieces scattered everywhere, you get anxious. You're unsure where to start, how to start, or even if you can start. This is the fear of starting. It's a sinking feeling in your stomach, a racing mind filled with "what ifs."

But why does this happen? The human brain naturally shies away from insurmountable tasks or those that require a great deal of effort and focus. When you have ADHD, your brain is already working overtime to navigate the complexities of everyday life. The thought of adding a large, demanding task to that mix seems terrifying. This fear often stems from a combination of executive function difficulties, past experiences with failure, and the overwhelming nature of large tasks. It's not procrastination; it's a deep-rooted fear of starting something new, possibly failing, and the mental energy needed to organize and execute the task.

It's okay to feel overwhelmed, and it's okay to fear the start. But don't let it control you. You are stronger, braver, and more capable than you think.

Past Failures

Remember that time when you tried to clean your entire home in a single day but ended up stressed out? And then there was the incident with the red wine stain on your white carpet. You started with a Google search on salt and stain removal and ended up on an infinite scroll of YouTube—2 hours later. It's a vicious cycle. The more disorganized your home, the more overwhelmed you feel. The more overwhelmed you feel, the harder it is to start. Each failed attempt further reinforces the belief that you can't do it. In truth, past failures are nothing more than learning experiences. They are the times you tried to tidy up, only to feel overwhelmed and give up midway. They are the days you managed to clean one room, only to find it back in chaos the next day. Experiences like these leave a stubborn stain on your morale, preventing you from trying again. But understand that past failures are just that—the past. While ADHD can make staying focused and organized harder, it's not impossible—every day is a new opportunity to try again. Past failures do not define your future. They are stepping stones, not roadblocks.

Overwhelm and Analysis Paralysis

Overwhelm is the feeling of being swamped, like a small boat in a stormy sea. It's the sense that there's too much to do and not enough time or energy to do it. It often stems from the brain's struggle to organize and process information efficiently. With ADHD, your mind races—juggling multiple thoughts at once, which is why you can't stay focused on a single task.

Analysis paralysis, on the other hand, is the inability to make decisions due to overthinking, excessive information, or choices. The paralysis comes from not being able to decide where to start cleaning or what method to use. It's like being stuck at a crossroads with a thousand different paths and no map.

These emotional barriers are more than just frustrating; they're exhausting. You're keenly aware of every spec of dust, every misplaced item, yet you're unsure where or how to start addressing it. And when you do try to start, the process feels disjointed and unproductive because you second guess every decision. Having ADHD is not just about dealing with hyperactivity or distraction; it's about navigating these emotional barriers. It's okay to feel overwhelmed, and it's okay to struggle with decisions. But you're more powerful than these feelings—and strategies and support are available to help you along the way.

REFRAMING AND ACCEPTANCE

Imagine you're a renowned artist gazing at a blank canvas. The room around you is cluttered, paint tubes strewn about, brushes piled high. But you, the artist, see beyond the mess. You see potential, a masterpiece waiting to happen.

This is reframing. Reframing is all about shifting your perspective into something more positive or achievable. Studies show that a positive outlook actually changes the brain's chemistry, reducing anxiety and promoting productivity (Chowdhury, 2019). So, when the negative emotions kick in, reframe them as an opportunity to declutter not just your surroundings but your mind, too.

Acceptance is your ally in this artistic adventure. It's easy to get frustrated with ourselves when we're not meeting perceived standards of cleanliness. But remember, everyone has their own pace and method. Don't be afraid to accept your unique way of doing things or how you feel while doing them. This acceptance helps lower the emotional stress tied to cleaning and improves mental well-being (Lindsay et al., 2018). So, embrace the whirlwind; don't fight it. The tornado of thoughts and the tsunami of tasks are not barriers but perspectives to change.

Shifting Perspectives

Have you ever tried seeing things from a different point of view? It's like swapping lenses on a camera—suddenly, the world takes on a new hue, revealing hidden layers of understanding. When you see things differently, you begin to realize having ADHD doesn't mean you're destined to live in clutter forever. To change your perspective, try to think of housekeeping less as a punishment and more like a step toward mastering your environment *and* your emotions:

- Think about the good feeling you'll get when you're done.
- Visualize your space, tidy and organized, and how much easier it will be to find things, to move, and to breathe.
- Don't see the pile of dishes as an overwhelming chore; think of it as a calming and rhythmic routine. Each dish you wash and dry is a small (but significant!) victory.
- Those times when vacuuming seems tedious, approach it as a workout—moving rhythmically back and forth around the furniture.
- Make dusting and decluttering an adventure. There is a story behind every household item you pick up. Use this as a chance to reminisce or decide whether you still need these items.

Even the most mundane tasks can become rewarding when we shift our perspective. When we view tasks as burdens, they become burdensome and tiresome. If we look at them differently and see opportunities for growth, learning, or even as a form of mindfulness or personal therapy, they become rewarding. What follows is a sense of accomplishment and a positive impact on our emotional state.

Mindfulness Practices

With mindfulness, you learn how to take the time to pay attention to the present moment without thinking about anything else. Instead of getting tangled in your to-do list or fretting over distractions, mindfulness encourages you to focus on the now. Let's say you're washing the dishes. But as usual, you get distracted from the task by a dozen other worries. This is where mindfulness steps in. Rather than getting pulled into the vortex of distractions, you guide your focus back to washing the dishes, immersing yourself in the sensory details:

- the sound of water splashing
- the sensation of soap bubbles
- the sight of dirt disappearing from the plates—these are all part of the process

You also have the freedom to let your mind wander. You don't need steadfast focus for this—let your thoughts drift, perhaps pondering on something as whimsical as what a life form made entirely of soap bubbles might look like. All it takes is re-channeling your focus:

- When decluttering, pay attention to the texture, weight, and color.

- While doing the laundry, sort it by colors, folding clothes, and enjoying the satisfaction of a job well done.
- Use the same approach for sweeping, dusting, or any other cleaning task. Notice the sound of the broom's bristles against the floor or the cloth's texture in your hand as you actively work to engage your senses and stay grounded in the moment.

Celebrating Effort Over Perfection

Perfectionism is a double-edged sword. On one hand, it drives you to achieve great things, but on the other, it can paralyze you with fear of not being "good enough." But let's flip the script and start celebrating effort over perfection. When you're facing a pile of dirty dishes in the kitchen sink:

- Perfectionism whispers, "You need to clean all of these perfectly, or you shouldn't even try."
- ADHD chimes in, "But there's so much; where do we even start?"
- Here's where celebrating your effort takes the stage. You say, "Let's just start with five dishes."

You roll up your sleeves, and you wash those five dishes. You didn't conquer the mountain, but you made a start, and that's worth celebrating!

Or picture your cluttered living room. Instead of letting perfectionism dictate that you clean and organize everything perfectly in one go, just pick up five things and put them away. You've made progress and put in the effort, and that's a win.

All it takes is resetting your mindset—you don't need to be perfect; you just need to try. Take baby steps, celebrate those steps, and gradually, you'll see that cluttered room transform into a well-organized space, and the intimidating pile of laundry becomes a tidy stack. The way to get through it is to remember your worth is not dictated by a spotless floor or a perfectly organized bookshelf. It's dictated by you, by your efforts, and your resilience.

SEEKING SUPPORT

Life's a rocky road, and no one's expected to sail through it alone. With ADHD, the walls keep shifting, and the end goal seems blurry. It's especially tough when it comes to tasks that require consistent focus. Sometimes, all you need is a helping hand or a listening ear to get you through the rough patches. Seeking support is not only okay, it's necessary and courageous. No, it doesn't mean you're weak; it's a testament to your strength and self-awareness in acknowledging the hurdles and actively seeking ways to overcome them. By reaching out to professional organizers, therapists, or even supportive friends, you're actively choosing to overcome your barriers to success.

But when do you know it's time to reach out for help? When you consistently find yourself struggling with everyday tasks, feeling overwhelmed, or when your emotional health starts to dip. You're not alone and reaching out for help is one of the smartest moves you can take toward better managing your ADHD. Don't ever shy away from seeking support. You're worth it!

Therapeutic Methods

Let's say you can't start on your laundry because it makes you feel overwhelmed. A common emotional barrier with ADHD is the fear of starting a task due to its perceived enormity (Nigg, 2021). But let's deal with this together.

Therapeutic methods like these are very helpful in managing overwhelming feelings:

- art and music therapy
- mindfulness

- dialectical behavior therapy (DBT)
- cognitive behavioral therapy (CBT)
- mindfulness-based cognitive therapy (MBCT)

They'll teach you to enhance your ability to focus on the present moment. Instead of seeing one huge pile, you'll concentrate on doing what needs to be done in that time. It doesn't seem that scary now, does it? Another emotional barrier is the fear of failure. You might think, *What if I never finish?* or *What if I mess up?* Through cognitive-behavioral techniques, you can learn to challenge these negative thoughts, replace them with positive affirmations, and develop a more resilient mindset. Therapy also promotes emotional regulation. When ADHD causes intense emotions, housekeeping can seem insurmountable. But with therapeutic methods, regulating these emotions becomes easier. You'll learn how to view housekeeping not as a punishment but as a way to create harmony in your home.

In the end, it comes down to letting yourself grow and learn through the process. Like any other task, housekeeping can be challenging, especially for those with ADHD. Therapeutic techniques are tools to help you overcome these challenges. It's about learning to navigate around these emotional barriers, not just bulldozing through them.

ADHD Coaching

Unlike therapy, which digs into your thought process and past experiences, ADHD coaching zeroes in on the here and now. It's an individualized and goal-oriented approach designed specifically to help you manage your day-to-day life.

An ADHD coach doesn't just tell you to clean up; instead, they work *with* you to understand how ADHD impacts this particular aspect of your life. Together, you'll pinpoint the specific challenges—maybe it's difficulty staying focused on a task, getting overwhelmed with where to start, or struggling with time management. Once you identify these issues, your coach will guide you in developing and implementing practical strategies to overcome these hurdles. Maybe it's breaking tasks down into manageable chunks, or perhaps it's finding a cleaning routine that works with your unique ADHD brain, not against it.

Getting this personalized support is easier than you might think. Many ADHD coaches offer services online, or you can ask your doctor to recommend someone.

Support Groups

There's nothing worse than feeling like you're the only one going through it. But in a support group, you meet others facing similar challenges. ADHD support groups empower you to tackle ADHD head-on and overcome the emotional barriers preventing you from sticking to a housekeeping routine. You'll get to learn from experience and, in turn, offer your own wisdom. They provide a safe, empathetic space where you can exchange experiences, share coping strategies, and receive practical advice for dealing with ADHD-related housekeeping issues. Think of it as a brainstorming session where you and others who understand your struggles can work together to make life easier.

Now, finding these groups is as easy as a quick internet search where you'll find:

- Children and Adults with Attention-Deficit/Hyperactivity Disorder (CHADD)
- Attention Deficit Disorder Association (ADDA)
- local hospitals
- community centers

Connecting with peers facing similar struggles regulates the brain's stress response. This is because social interaction promotes the production of the hormone oxytocin, which has a calming effect and reduces stress levels (Uvnäs-Moberg & Petersson, 2005). Group support also improves self-esteem—and the best part?

You'll make new friends! A supportive network of like-minded peers motivates you to stay on track.

FROM EMOTIONAL PARALYSIS TO CLEANING EMPOWERMENT

Meet Angelo, a vibrant young man whose life has been marked by the peaks and troughs of ADHD emotional paralysis. But Angelo's story isn't about defeat; it's about transformation, empowerment, and, most importantly, self-discovery.

Angelo recalls his moment of realization, "My mother tripped over my football gear. She wasn't badly hurt but it was a wake-up call." Inspired by this moment, Angelo got help from a therapist and confronted his emotional issues head-on. It wasn't easy, but Angelo was resolute. His transformation was slow but steady. He started with small tasks, like wiping the mirrors down and making his bed every day. Soon, he was able to clear the dishes from the sink and then the clutter from the living room. As time went on, he moved on to bigger jobs, tackling one zone at a time. "Each day," he says, "I could physically see my progress. It was like clearing the cobwebs from my mind, too."

Cleaning his home was not the only thing Angelo was doing; he was also cleaning his emotions, gradually removing the dust of past traumas. Angelo's journey wasn't smooth; there were setbacks and days of relapse into old habits. But he never gave up and finally took control of his life and his home. Today, Angelo and his mother live in a clean, clutter-free environment, a testament to his victory over emotional paralysis.

Angelo's story is one of resilience and determination. It emphasizes that no matter how overpowering emotional hurdles might be, you can always find the strength to overcome them, even in the unlikeliest of places—a cluttered house.

Key takeaway: Overcoming emotional barriers linked to ADHD and housekeeping isn't an overnight process, but with persistence and resolve, you can definitely make significant strides. Addressing emotional barriers is a big deal, but it's only part of a broader journey to emotional well-being. It's equally valuable to cultivate consistent habits and work toward long-term change and growth.

Helping Other People Find Their Organizational Superpowers

"Everyone shines, given the right lighting."

— SUSAN CAIN

One of the most commonly cited difficulties for people with ADHD is the struggle to stay organized ... but this isn't because they're inherently *dis*organized. It's because the challenge to stay focused makes it hard to stay on top of everything.

You're discovering how your ADHD can be a superpower for maintaining a tidy home when you have the right strategies, but not many people realize that, let alone know how to find those strategies.

There are many people out there who do their best to keep their ADHD under wraps, desperately trying to fit themselves as a square peg into a round hole, and if you've ever done this, you'll know that it doesn't work. The secret lies in embracing who you truly are and then looking at how you can make that work for you. You can do this in all areas of life, but my mission with this book is to focus on whipping your home into shape— for the simple reason that a calm home has a huge impact on your ability to calm your mind when it's racing.

It's my goal to share these strategies with as many people with ADHD as I can ... and I'd like to take this opportunity to ask for your help.

By leaving a review of this book on Amazon, you'll lead anyone searching for advice on how to organize their home with an ADHD brain to the tools and techniques that will help them.

Every review acts as a signpost to help new readers find the guidance they're looking for. Helping someone else to transform their experience of cleaning and tidying really is as simple as that.

Thank you so much for your support. It's more powerful than you realize.

6

BUILDING AND MAINTAINING HABITS

Building and maintaining habits is like cultivating a garden. Just as a plant needs consistent care, not sporadic watering, our habits require regular attention and effort. Each habit is a seedling; the daily nurturing is the sunlight and water it needs to grow. Occasional commitment, like occasional watering, might keep it alive but won't let it flourish. Over time, with consistency and patience, these seedlings transform into sturdy trees, bearing the fruits of our discipline and hard work. They become a part of our life's landscape, providing shade and sustenance, just like well-formed habits offer structure and routine.

THE POWER OF ROUTINE

When we establish routines, we create a clear, predictable pattern that helps our brain know what's coming next. With ADHD, it's even more important. Routine is your gravity. One that pulls erratic thoughts into a steady, automatic rhythm, helping you manage time and stay organized by reducing the number of decisions you have to make during the day. Routine is your brain's best friend, offering the chance for:

- streamlined tasks
- increased productivity
- reduced stress
- security and control
- better time management
- improved physical and mental health

Imagine not having to decide what comes next or forget important tasks and deadlines. That's the power of routine. It's not about rigidity but creating a safety net that allows you to take risks and be creative and spontaneous without the constant fear of dropping the ball.

Routines are not one-size-fits-all. What works for one person might not work for another. To find out what works for you and your ADHD traits, check out these powerful techniques you can incorporate into your daily routine.

Habit Stacking

Habit stacking is a fundamental principle of the *Atomic Habits* (2018) methodology made popular by James Clear. In his pioneering book on habit formation, Clear discusses several strategies for building effective routines, and habit stacking is one of them. The concept of habit stacking involves pairing a new habit with an existing one, which makes it easier to incorporate more tasks into your routine. This principle works by utilizing the existing neural networks in our brains, making habit formation more effective and sustainable. It's like building a tower with Lego bricks, where each brick represents a different habit. They don't have to be big, immediate changes but gradual, consistent improvements. The compound effect, popularized by bestselling author Darren Hardy, highlights real change comes from the effect of hundreds of small decisions. Collectively, these small habits, actions, and routines lead to significant life changes (Hardy, 2010).

Let's consider habit stacking to make a routine around housekeeping:

1. Begin with something easy, like making the bed in the morning.

2. Now, how about adding a new habit to that? Once your bed is made, immediately start a load of laundry. This is the "stacked" part of your habit stack.
3. After a few days, this pair of actions will start to feel like a single, seamless habit.
4. When that happens, add another habit on top. Maybe after starting the laundry, you can spend 10 minutes decluttering one area of your home.

Before you know it, you've created a powerful morning routine that keeps your home neat and tidy. And the best part? You've done it without needing to make a bunch of conscious decisions or exert a lot of willpower.

Now you've found your rhythm, let's kick things up a notch by introducing "anchoring habits," a strategy where you use existing habits as a foundation to amplify the efficiency of your routine.

Anchoring Habits

Think of anchor habits as the solid roots of a tree. These are habits so established in your routine that you perform them without a second thought, like brushing your teeth, having your morning coffee, or walking the dog. You do these tasks automatically, right?

Now, imagine if you could use these anchor habits to create new, productive routines. That's the magic of anchor habits! You can use them as a springboard for developing other habits. Because our brains have a knack for recognizing patterns and creating associations, consistently pairing one habit with another, you're training your brain to adapt automatically. As an example, if you already read a book before bed, you can use that habit as an anchor to build a new habit of decluttering your bedside table. Just start immediately before or after reading. By piggybacking on these deeply rooted habits, new routines become easier to remember. It's like adding a new branch to an already strong tree. The key is to start small and grow gradually:

- After brushing your teeth in the morning (existing habit), immediately wipe down the bathroom counter (new habit).
- Once you finish breakfast (existing habit), make it a habit to wash the bowl right away (new habit).
- When you get up from your desk for a lunch break (existing habit), take a moment to declutter and organize your workspace (new habit).

Now, let's apply this anchoring concept to your ADHD traits—finding a routine compatible with your unique characteristics is just as significant.

ADHD and Routine Compatibility

The ADHD brain thrives on stimulation. When it lacks stimulation, it tends to wander. You start cleaning the living room, then notice the dirty countertops, and before you know it, you've moved on to the bathroom, leaving each task half-done. Routine compatibility means finding a routine that works with your specific traits rather than against them. No more forcing yourself into a rigid structure that doesn't fit. All it takes is understanding your strengths and weaknesses and identifying what works best for you:

- If you're a night owl, don't force yourself into a morning routine. Instead, create a routine that takes advantage of your peak energy times.
- If you lose motivation, make your routine stimulating and include activities you enjoy to keep your brain engaged.
- If you're easily distracted, try breaking down tasks into smaller, manageable chunks.
- If you have frequent bouts of hyperfocus, use that energy to tackle cleaning tasks head-on.

- If you're forgetful, set reminders or use apps to keep you on track.
- If you're an extrovert, get your friends involved and host a cleaning party.

Next up in your new habits-building arsenal is the cue-routine-reward cycle. This psychological model might be just what you need to tailor your routine around your ADHD, building a rewarding system that works.

CUE-ROUTINE-REWARD CYCLE

The cue-routine-reward cycle, also known as the habit loop, is a neurobiological phenomenon first identified and articulated by Charles Duhigg in his book *The Power of Habit* (Duhigg, 2012). The clear structure of this cycle provides a straightforward pathway to habit formation, making it easier to deal with impulsivity and focus issues.

1. **Cue:** The cycle begins with a cue. This is a trigger that tells your brain to go into automatic mode. It could be anything from a time of day, a location, or an emotional state.
2. **Routine:** Then there's the routine, which is the action you perform, either physical, mental, or emotional.

3. **Reward:** Finally, there's the reward, which helps your brain remember this pattern for the future.

The science behind the impact of this cycle is rooted in our brain chemistry. Every time we perform a routine after recognizing a cue and receiving a reward, our brains release dopamine—a feel-good hormone. This makes us want to repeat the action, creating a habit, after the neural pathways associated with the habit become stronger and more automatic (Mwewa, 2023).

Understanding the cue-routine-reward cycle is just the beginning. The real breakthrough comes when we learn to recognize these cues that trigger the cycle so we can take control and shape our habits better.

Recognizing Cues

Cues are powerful triggers that set off a chain of actions. For example, if your cluttered coffee table triggers a feeling of restlessness, that's your cue! It's your brain telling you it's time to roll up your sleeves and get cleaning. To get a better feel for these cues, pay attention to your surroundings and the emotions they evoke.

- Does a pile of unwashed dishes make you anxious?

- Does an untidy living room make you feel overwhelmed?

Now, imagine this: Every time you finish a cup of coffee, you see the empty mug as a cue to immediately wash it instead of letting it pile up. Or whenever you see dust accumulating on your bookshelf, you take it as a cue to give it a quick wipe-down.

These are your trigger cues. They're the signals your brain sends to get you moving, prompting a specific action in response. Now, onto routines—the heart of the cue-routine-reward cycle.

Establishing Routines

Once you've recognized your cues, the next step is to establish a routine to address them. Let's go back to the cue of the cluttered coffee table. Your routine to address this cue is to spend 5 minutes clearing it off and wiping it down. Don't be embarrassed to take it slow and steady. After all, habit-forming is most likely to happen with small, manageable tasks since they're easier to repeat consistently and require less effort (Gardner, 2012).

- **Cue:** A full laundry basket (overwhelmed).
  Routine: Do the laundry in half loads.

- **Cue:** Dirty dishes in the sink (frustration). **Routine:** After dinner, immediately wash the dishes or load them into the dishwasher.
- **Cue:** Dust on furniture (irritation). **Routine:** Grab a dust cloth and give the furniture a quick wipe down.

It's easy enough to get the hang of things once you know how to recognize negative feelings and then establish a consistent routine in response to them. Remember, routines aren't set in stone. They're flexible. If one routine isn't working for you, feel free to tweak it or try something else. Finding a routine that suits you and your lifestyle is how you stay consistent.

Once you've nailed down a routine that fits seamlessly into your life, it's time to sweeten the deal by setting up a reward—after all, who doesn't love a good treat for a job well done? This is the next essential step in nurturing your new habits and making them stick.

Setting up Satisfying Rewards

Rewards are the crowning glory, the light at the end of the cleaning tunnel. They're what makes the cue-routine-reward cycle worth it and they come after you're done with the routine. The reward can be anything:

- the satisfaction of maintaining a clean space
- a well-deserved 15-minute break
- the aesthetic pleasure of a tidy environment
- the mental clarity that comes from removing clutter
- a present from yourself after a week of sticking to your new routine

They don't have to be big or extravagant. They can be as simple as taking a moment to appreciate your clean and tidy space or giving yourself permission to do something you love. The key is to choose rewards that are meaningful to you—whatever makes you feel good.

The power of the cue-routine-reward cycle lies in its simplicity and its universality. Habits, good or bad, all follow this cycle. It's your job now to understand and harness this pattern to form healthier and more productive habits and to break away from harmful or unproductive ones. By consciously associating specific cues to desirable routines and rewarding outcomes, you'll rewire your unique ADHD brain to automatically follow these new, improved patterns of behavior. This is the essence of habit formation and the key to taking control of your habits and, by extension, your life.

However, even with the best intentions, the most solid routines aren't immune to occasional hiccups. It's in these moments of slip-ups where the true test lies. Learning to address them will fortify your habit-formation journey, keeping you on track toward shaping a calmer home and mind.

ADDRESSING SLIPS

We all have those days when our routines fly out the window:

- getting distracted by a TV show and leaving the dishes in the sink overnight
- ignoring the full laundry basket while dirty clothes pile up
- cleaning only visible areas and neglecting hidden spots so grime builds

It's easy to beat yourself up over it, to feel like you've failed somehow because you didn't stick to your routine. But here's the thing: you haven't. Life is unpredictable, and sometimes, we need to roll with the punches.

Having a tidy home is fantastic, but it's not the be-all and end-all. What truly matters is your happiness and peace. So, if you slipped up, give yourself a break. You're human, and it's okay to have off days—progress is more important than perfection. Maybe today was a slip-up, but tomorrow is a brand-new day to get back on track. Instead of dwelling on a missed step, learn from it and remember that self-compassion is the way to long-term success.

Being Kind to Oneself

You are doing great! I just needed to say that up front because it's easy to forget. You're managing your ADHD, trying to keep up with housekeeping, organizing, and everything else. But guess what? It's perfectly okay to fall short.

Life isn't a straight path. It's more like a zigzag, full of unexpected turns, hurdles, and, yes, even a few slip-ups. Sometimes, you'll miss a day of cleaning, or your routine takes a backseat because something else crops up. It happens. But here's the thing: You don't need to be hard on yourself. Being kind to yourself doesn't mean always doing everything perfectly; it means understanding that perfection is an illusion and it's fine not to be "on" all the time. Being kind to yourself means giving yourself grace when things don't go as planned and not using those moments as a reason to berate yourself.

If you slip up, don't spiral into self-criticism; pause for a moment. Take a deep breath and remind yourself that you're human and that humans are entitled to make mistakes. Recognize that your worth is not tied to how clean your house is or how organized your life seems—you're much more than that.

So, how can you be kind to yourself? It's pretty straightforward.

1. Acknowledge your efforts. You're tackling your ADHD and doing your best to maintain a routine—that's commendable.
2. Give yourself permission to learn and grow from your slip-ups instead of dwelling on them.
3. Remember, each day is a new opportunity. If yesterday was rough, today could be better. And even if it's not, that's okay, too.

Cut yourself some slack, adjust your expectations, and most importantly, remind yourself regularly: You're doing your best, and your best is more than enough.

Being kind to yourself also means giving yourself the room to analyze where things went wrong. So, let's dive in and dissect those slip-ups, recognizing them not as failures but as stepping stones to build a more effective routine.

Analyzing the Slip

Let's say you've been on a roll with your cleaning routine—the dishes have been done daily, the floors are sparkling, and the clutter is under control. But then, one day, you're surrounded by a mess again. What happened? Chances are, a change in your routine or environment led to this slip-up. Maybe you had guests over or a hectic week at work.

Think of it like this: These slip-ups aren't failures; they're data. Your brain works differently with ADHD. You're more sensitive to changes and disruptions, and your energy levels can fluctuate wildly. So, when a slip-up happens, it's not a reflection of your worth or ability; it's valuable information about what circumstances or triggers make it harder for you to stick to your habits.

The next time you find yourself in a slip-up situation, take a moment to analyze:

1. What changed?
2. What was different about this day, this week, this month?
3. Were there any external stressors that might have contributed?
4. And most importantly, how did you feel? Were you tired, overwhelmed, distracted?

Being aware of these factors will give you a clearer perspective of the problem. Then, you can create an action plan to avoid or better handle similar circumstances to prevent future slip-ups. It all starts by making thoughtful adjustments.

Tweaking for Success

Tweaking for success is not about drastic changes but rather the subtle, deliberate adjustments you make in response to your slip-ups.

Here are some common missteps and some tweaks to prevent them from happening again. Keep in mind your specific ADHD traits—these are just suggestions. What works best for you might be different. So, feel free to experiment and modify these suggestions to suit you.

- **Forgetting to clean:** The tweak here would be to set alarms or reminders on your phone to go off at specific times during the day.
- **Leaving tasks half-done:** To fix this, put on some music, listen to a podcast, chunk the job down into zone by zone, or even just one part of a room.
- **Procrastinating on big tasks:** The tweak here is to start small. Aim to clean for just 15

minutes. Once you've started, you'll find it easier to keep going.

- **Neglecting regular maintenance chores:** To remember these, use a planner or a digital scheduling tool to remind you when these chores are due.

So, there you have it. Tweaking your habits and routines goes beyond making chores easier—making adjustments involves turning them into opportunities for success *tailored* to your ADHD journey. Still need convincing? Let's take a detour into the lives of Alex and Sam—one has formed habits, the other hasn't. You'll see how their stories underline the significant impact routine has on their life and housekeeping with ADHD.

ADHD AND HABITS: TWO CASES

Sam and Alex—their experiences with ADHD, particularly with housekeeping, were as different as chalk and cheese.

Sam developed a system of habits and routines, a coping mechanism, to manage his ADHD and keep his home in order. Each morning, he'd start his day with a detailed to-do list, breaking down tasks into manageable chunks.

Making the bed? That was a non-negotiable first thing. Dishes were dealt with right after meals so they wouldn't pile up. Evening time was reserved for a quick tidy-up. His routines were predictable and this consistency helped him manage his impulsivity and inattention.

Now, let's turn to Alex. Unlike Sam, Alex hadn't embraced any form of routine or habit. His home was a constant jumble of clutter and disarray. In this disorderly environment, distractibility and forgetfulness only worsened. Most of the time, he lost things in the clutter, which made him more frustrated and anxious. Alex knew of Sam's calm lifestyle and couldn't help but yearn for the same. Observing Sam, he realized that habits and routines weren't shackles but tools for dealing with ADHD and keeping the house in order. Encouraged by Sam's success, Alex began to experiment with his own routines. He started small, putting his clothes into the laundry basket as soon as he took them off and setting aside specific times for vacuuming and tidying up. Gradually, he added more complex habits, like giving his appliances a quick wipe-down after putting the laundry on and dusting off the surface after organizing a pile of books.

Soon enough, Alex noticed his mind was less chaotic, and he found it easier to focus on what needed to be done. He could manage his time more effectively and was less prone to procrastination.

So, you see, ADHD may come with its set of challenges, but as Sam showed, habits and routines are powerful allies. They provide structure, reduce stress, and pave the way for better housekeeping. And as Alex learned, it's never too late to start.

Key takeaway: The transformative power of routine, habit stacking, and anchoring habits carve a path toward a calmer home and mind. As you steadily establish housekeeping habits and routines, you'll find they are essential to creating an ADHD-friendly home environment. With this, order and predictability not only complement your unique brain wiring but also greatly enhance your productivity and peace of mind.

7

DESIGNING AN ADHD-FRIENDLY HOME ENVIRONMENT

Have you ever thought about the invisible hand constantly sculpting our behavior, decisions, and, ultimately, our lives? No, it's not some supernatural force or a secret society—it's the environment we live in. Our surroundings, often unnoticed, influence us greatly. Think about how your home fits into this. It can either facilitate focus and productivity or breed chaos, especially when dealing with ADHD. With this in mind, let's take a closer look at exactly how you can design your home environment *tailored* to your ADHD.

DECLUTTERING

Clutter overstimulates the brain, triggering mental fatigue—each item in your field of vision pulls at your attention little by little. When you minimize clutter, you reduce the number of stimuli competing for attention, making it easier to concentrate. As a visual diet, with decluttering, you're cutting down on the "junk" clogging up your mental space, making room for more focus. And that's a big win in creating an ADHD-friendly home.

ADHD-Friendly Decluttering Methods

The traditional methods of decluttering often don't work; they're too rigid and too structured. They don't consider the *unique* way your brain processes information. What you need are ADHD-friendly decluttering methods backed by science.

- **Color-coding:** People with ADHD respond well to the organizational benefits of visual stimuli (Park, 2013). Use a color-coding system to assign different colors to categories of items. For example, red for important paperwork, blue for everyday household items, and green for personal belongings.
- **Daily decluttering sessions:** Based on the Pomodoro Technique, break your tasks into 25-minute chunks, followed by a 5-minute break. How does it work? Short, focused bursts of

activity are better for ADHD brains (Drake, 2021).

- **One room at a time:** Focus on one zone at a time to align with the ADHD brain's need for instant gratification (Littman, 2017). For this to work, it's helpful to start with the room causing the most stress or distraction—you'll see tangible progress quickly, which boosts motivation to tackle other areas.

These techniques are designed with your ADHD brain in mind. They're flexible, intuitive, and focus on your strengths, like creativity and spontaneity. So, ditch the one-size-fits-all methods and embrace a decluttering system that respects and harnesses your ADHD superpowers.

Importance of Clear Spaces

ADHD-friendly decluttering and clear spaces are two sides of the same coin, working hand in hand to make your life better.

You know that feeling when you walk into an open, clear room? It's refreshing, isn't it? It's like a physical manifestation of a mental reset. The uncluttered space allows your mind to relax, reduces stress, and increases your ability to focus (Phillips, 2023). For ADHD, this sensation is even more profound. Clean and organized spaces promote a healthier and more productive working environment by reducing distractions and making it easier to concentrate. This isn't all. A clear space is more than just a sign of good housekeeping. When you minimize clutter, you reduce the surfaces where dust and allergens settle. Consequently, by maintaining a clear space, you're promoting a healthier living environment.

But here's the icing on the cake: Clear spaces encourage decluttering. Seeing the benefits of a decluttered space motivates you to keep it that way. The reason for this is that you've gained self-confidence. A well-organized space gives you a sense of accomplishment and pride, contributing to your overall well-being.

The takeaway? Clear spaces in the home are not just pleasing to the eye—they're beneficial for your mental health, housekeeping, and productivity. Now, the question is, what should you keep and what should you get rid of to achieve this clutter-free haven?

Items to Keep vs. Discard

If every item in your home has a purpose and a place, then you're on the right track to home bliss. That's the heart of the "Items to keep vs. discard" method. It's all about figuring out how valuable each item is. You take a pile of unworn clothes, your horde of "important" papers, your mismatch of miscellaneous items you're positive you'll need one day and ask, "Do I really need this? Is it useful?" If your answer is a resounding *yes*, it stays. If the response is a shrug or a "not really," it's time to say goodbye.

- **The joy check:** Marie Kondo, a renowned decluttering expert, swears by this method. Hold each item in your hands and ask yourself, *Does this spark joy?* If it does, keep it. If it doesn't, thank it for its service and let it go.
- **The 365-day rule:** Your home is not a museum for unused items. Haven't used an item in the last year? You probably don't need it. This rule is fantastic for things like clothes, kitchen gadgets, or books.
- **The 10-second rule:** Grab an item and give yourself 10 seconds to decide its fate—trust your gut. Making quick decisions using this method prevents you from overthinking.

Any of these keep vs. discard methods makes it so you're not mindlessly discarding items but mindfully curating a space with a purpose. Think of it as a lifestyle choice linking simplicity and mindfulness with the goal of enhancing your well-being.

Designing an ADHD-friendly home requires more than decluttering, though. The idea is to use color, texture, and light in a way that energizes or calms you, depending on your mood—as well as choosing furniture and storage solutions that make sense for your habits and routines.

ORGANIZATIONAL SYSTEMS

If the brain is a busy city, the streets are the neural pathways, and the traffic is the thoughts zipping along. But when you have ADHD, it's like all your city's traffic lights are flashing yellow—it's chaos! Here's where ADHD-specific organizational systems come in. These systems, when implemented within a home, act like traffic lights, guiding and controlling the flow of thoughts, tasks, and activities. They work by bringing structure, predictability, and regularity into your environment, which is incredibly soothing for an ADHD brain.

Visual Storage Solutions

"A place for everything, and everything in its place." This is a poignant saying when it comes to designing an ADHD-friendly home. Which, by the way, is an extension of your personality, a reflection of your taste. And what better way to show this off than with visual storage solutions? Use them to organize your space, making it more functional and easier to navigate—no more tripping over shoes! They also enhance the aesthetics of your home—imagine a sleek bookshelf of your favorite novels or a tastefully designed box for your keepsakes.

- **Floating shelves:** Excellent for displaying books, ornaments, or kitchen essentials. Mount them on the wall to free up floor space and give your room a stylish touch.
- **Over-the-door organizers:** Use these to store items like shoes, accessories, toiletries, or anything else clogging up your home.
- **Ready-to-hang systems:** These customizable storage solutions come as wall-mounted shelves, racks, hooks, bins, and other storage components.
- **Magnetic boards:** Used to store magnetic items or items with magnetic clips, they're ideal for displaying important notes, photos, and reminders.
- **Decorative baskets and bins:** These come in different shapes, sizes, and materials like wicker, metal, plastic, or fabric and can hold anything from toys, books, and clothes to

kitchen utensils. You can color-code them and use labels to identify what goes where.

No matter what type of visual storage you choose, try to stay on top of keeping them organized, too. Nothing too arduous, just a monthly check-in to make sure the items are still useful. If not, use your favorite decluttering method for a quick tidy-up.

Now, let's take organization a notch higher—enter labeling and categorizing.

Labeling and Categorizing

With labeling and categorizing, you'll know exactly where everything is, saving you precious time and unnecessary stress. It's a small effort upfront that pays off big time in the long run. When you label and categorize, you set clear boundaries for where everything goes:

- Let's start in the kitchen. Don't just shove everything into cupboards—categorize items based on the frequency of use or by function. Daily dishes on reachable shelves, baking supplies together, and so on. Group everything accordingly, and label each shelf or container: "tins," "cereal," and "snacks." Now, every time you unload your groceries, you'll know exactly where everything goes.

But don't just stop at the kitchen. You can apply this method all over your home—label and categorize everything from jars to boxes to files. Knowing where stuff is isn't enough; it's also knowing where it goes.

- **Garage:** Group your tools, gardening equipment, and car products.
- **Home office:** Group and label your paperwork —"bills," "work documents," "kids' school papers," and so on.
- **Wardrobe:** Label your drawers or sections: "socks," "underwear," and "T-shirts."
- **Drawers:** Instead of a mountain of mystery boxes, you've got clearly marked storage like "letters," "miscellaneous," "household items," and "kids' stuff."

Once you've mastered labeling and categorizing, step up your game with simplified organizing—a natural progression that streamlines your system.

Simplified Organizing

Simplified home organizing is about creating an environment that minimizes distractions and maximizes functionality. Easy-to-navigate spaces, clearly labeled storage, and a place for everything turn a chaotic environment into a calm one. If you struggle with focus and distraction, then simplicity is for you. Besides making life easier, it'll boost productivity and reduce stress.

Simplified organizing in a nutshell:

1. Declutter.
2. Organize.
3. Simplify.

How to do it:

- **Go digital:** Paper clutter is a real thing. Digitize documents and photos, and unsubscribe from physical mail.
- **Don't delay; do it now:** Put things back where they belong as soon as you're done with them.
- **Use vertical spaces:** Shelves, hooks, and hanging organizers free up a lot of floor and counter space.
- **Streamline your storage:** Invest in smart storage solutions. You don't need a whole wall of cabinets—instead, think of multi-purpose furniture like ottomans with hidden storage or beds with drawers underneath.

- **Simplify your wardrobe:** Sort through your clothes and only keep what you love and wear often.
- **Create a place for everything:** Have a specific place for all your items. If it helps, label the storage areas.
- **Keep flat surfaces clear:** Make it a rule to keep surfaces like counters and tables as clear as possible.
- **Set up a donation station:** Have a box or bag to quickly toss items you no longer need. Once it's full, donate the contents to a charity.

Are you drawn to the idea of simplified organizing? Consider this: Minimalism is like simplified organizing turbo-charged.

MINIMALISM AND ADHD

The design of your home has a profound effect on your ADHD symptoms. Research suggests that cluttered environments exacerbate anxiety and restlessness, common features of ADHD (Livingstone et al., 2016). Therein lies the power of minimalism.

It's a design philosophy born in the 1960s, emphasizing simplicity and functionality. It's like a breath of fresh air, focusing on quality over quantity. Using minimalism in your home means paring down to the essentials, decluttering spaces, and using streamlined, functional storage and furniture. Minimalism doesn't mean living without; it means living intentionally. This principle applies to everything from furniture to decor.

Benefits of Fewer Distractions

Our brains like order, so constant visual reminders of disorganization drain our cognitive resources, reducing our ability to focus (McMains & Kastner, 2011). In other words, simplifying your home to only the essentials makes it ADHD-friendly.

If your home is too cluttered, too noisy, or simply too much, then minimalism—the art of living with less, will benefit you and your ADHD:

- **Reduces visual clutter:** By simplifying your environment, you create a tranquil environment that enhances focus and alleviates ADHD symptoms.
- **Promotes better organization:** Fewer items mean less cleaning and organizing, thus reducing ADHD-related stress, and promoting better organization.
- **Enhances engagement and focus:** Some adults with ADHD engage better and focus more in

environments with fewer distractions (Canela et al., 2017).

- **Ensures peace and calm:** A minimalist home is like an uncluttered retreat from daily stress, especially beneficial when struggling with overstimulation.

Minimalism beautifully strips away the unnecessary, leaving you with more time to devote to what matters most. Now, imagine applying this concept to your entire life, not just your surroundings.

Embracing Essentialism

Essentialism is like minimalism's twin flame. A philosophy that, when combined with minimalism, will make your life, especially your home environment, simpler and more meaningful. The idea of essentialism centers around making the most of your time and energy by only doing things that align with your core values. This means getting rid of distractions and unnecessary choices. Aligning perfectly with the tenets of minimalism—the practice of living with less, both philosophies encourage you to reduce possessions, declutter your space, and live a life of intentionality.

But how does this work? Take a look around your home. Is there anything in your home that you rarely use or doesn't make you happy? Essentialism asks you to evaluate each item critically and keep only what you need. Ask yourself, "Is this essential? Does it have a purpose?" If the answer is no, then get rid of it by donating, selling, or throwing it away.

The Freedom of Less

The allure of "the freedom of less" is gaining momentum, and for good reason. When you let go of the nonessentials, you create space for what counts. An unburdened sense of liberation is formed from this simplicity, a profoundly enriching freedom. Graham Hill, a renowned advocate of minimalist living, says, "My space is small. My life is big" (Hill, 2013). And he's onto something. Studies on materialism in the American Psychological Association show that people with fewer possessions are generally happier and less stressed. Less truly can be more.

Now, don't get the wrong impression. Living with less doesn't mean you have to give up everything you love; instead, make conscious choices about what you have in your home by asking "why" you have it. The results? Well, you'll have less cleaning, less stress, more time, more freedom, and more satisfaction.

Interestingly, this lifestyle has seen a surge in popularity recently. Maybe you've seen the Netflix series *Tidying Up with Marie Kondo* or heard about

Scandinavian minimalist living. Why the attraction? Because there's real, tangible value in it—the benefits of embracing "the freedom of less" go beyond the physical. It's a mental and emotional shift as well.

CASE STUDY: A COMPLETE TRANSFORMATION

Jane, a mother of two, recently transformed her home to cater to her son's ADHD. Jane's son, Mark, struggled with focus, was easily distracted, and often misplaced things. His school performance was declining, and daily life was a battle. Jane realized Mark's environment might be contributing to his challenges, so she created an ADHD-friendly environment. Starting with Mark's bedroom, she used soft, soothing colors for the walls and utilized natural light to keep the room bright and airy. She also minimized clutter and kept furniture to a minimum, making Mark's room feel and look spacious. She then turned to the rest of the house. She designated specific areas for different activities—a quiet corner for his books, a table for his homework, and only the living room for TV and games. She used clear, labeled storage bins to help Mark keep track of his things. The results were astonishing. Mark became more focused, had an easier time finding things, and performed better in school. He also seemed happier and more relaxed.

What Jane's story teaches us is that our environment greatly impacts our behavior and well-being, especially with ADHD. By making a few changes here and there, you can create a home that promotes calm, minimizes distractions, and promotes focus. Just like Jane, you might be surprised at the difference it makes.

Key takeaway: Designing an ADHD-friendly home is more than an assignment; it's an opportunity for you to take control and transform your living space into a sanctuary of peace and productivity. Now you know how to optimize your home, how can you ensure long-term success? It's time to move beyond your immediate environment and explore the concept of continuous growth.

8

LONG-TERM STRATEGIES AND CONTINUAL GROWTH

How can the ADHD brain maintain a tidy home forever? Well, your long-term strategies guide your actions and decisions. In your case, this would be the fight toward creating sustainable habits. Maybe it's a daily to-do list or a weekly cleaning schedule. Whatever it is, it's a plan that sets your pace and rhythm.

Continual growth relies on learning and adapting. Your ADHD brain is exceptionally adaptive, thriving on novelty and new experiences (Sedgwick et al., 2018). This means you're perfectly positioned to use this flexibility to your advantage! How? By continuously seeking and learning new methods and strategies to keep your home clean and tidy.

Even so, the pursuit of improvement involves more than moving forward; it's equally valuable to hit the pause button, step back, and reflect on your progress.

REVIEW AND REFLECT

Think of this as a self-audit—you're evaluating your performance, pinpointing areas of improvement. This doesn't mean nitpicking every dust particle you might've missed or berating yourself for skipping a week, but rather making sure you're on the right track. When reviewing and reflecting, think about your newly formed habits and routines:

- Do they help you work better?
- Were there tasks that took longer than expected, so you got distracted?
- Areas that were dirtier than you thought, so you need to take things slower?
- Did you overlook certain tasks or not follow through on them?

This is the moment to analyze your routine, understand its shortcomings, and figure out where you can make improvements. Remember the aim is to always make your routine ADHD-friendly, and then create a structure to support them based on the techniques you've learned so far.

Reflection is the key to evolution. It brings mindfulness into the equation. You aren't just sweeping through tasks mindlessly—you're aware of your actions, challenges, and triumphs. And just as you pause to consider your cleaning routine, it's equally important to have those monthly check-ins.

Monthly Check-Ins

Use a monthly check-in as your personal progress report. Here, you'll sit down each month to review your cleaning habits, evaluate what's working and what's not, and adjust accordingly.

- **Self-assess:** Take a look around your home, noting areas that feel cluttered, dirty, or disorganized. If you're consistently struggling with the same areas, adjust your routine to fit these areas.
- **Cleanliness level:** If you still have dust, grime, or unclean dishes, you might need to change the amount of time you spend on your cleaning habits.
- **Time management:** Make sure you're not procrastinating because your cleaning tasks are

overwhelming. If you are, chunk them into smaller, manageable tasks.

- **Routine consistency:** Have you been sticking to your routine? If not, identify the barriers and go back to Chapter 5 to find ways to overcome them.
- **Emotional well-being:** Never underestimate the effect your emotions have on how you perform. If the routine makes you stressed or anxious, change it to suit your comfort level.

Monthly check-ins allow for trial and error. So, throughout the ebbs and flows of life, you're naturally primed to tackle new challenges head-on.

Addressing New Challenges

With ADHD, new routines, like a housekeeping schedule, pose unique challenges. This is a natural transition as you adjust to maintaining focus, managing time, and staying organized. But here's the thing—you can conquer them through adaptation and planning. The more you learn and adapt, the more you refine your housekeeping skills! Here's how to deal with challenges:

Distractions

- **Solution:** Create a distraction-free zone when cleaning. Put your phone on silent and focus on one task at a time.

Time management

- **Solution:** Use timers or alarms to keep you on track and divide chores into achievable chunks.

Changes in routine

- **Solution:** Gradually introduce changes and jazz things up visually with a colorful wall planner or get out your cleaning playlist.

Organizational difficulties

- **Solution:** Use clear, labeled containers for each category of items.

Memory issues

- **Solution:** Use the checklist at the end of this book to stay on track

Overwhelm

- **Solution:** Split chores into simpler steps.

Lack of motivation

- **Solution:** Reward yourself after completing tasks or turn cleaning into a game to make it more fun.

Impulsivity

- **Solution:** Focus on completing one job at a time before moving on to the next.

Hyperfocus

- **Solution:** Set reminders to switch tasks so all your chores get equal attention.

Fatigue

- **Solution:** Schedule breaks and rest periods during your routine.

Perfectionism

- **Solution:** Tell yourself it's okay for your home to be "clean enough." Don't let perfectionism hinder your progress.

Meeting new challenges head-on is only half the story. In the other half, we celebrate our accomplishments, acknowledge our progress, and fuel our future endeavors with that energy.

Celebrating Progress

With housekeeping, it's easy enough to focus on what's left to be done and ignore what you have done. But you need to recognize and celebrate the small and big wins. This means stepping back, taking a breather, and saying, "Hey, I've done well!"

Let's take an example—you've been taking small steps to reduce mess in your bedroom. As time goes on, you've managed to completely transform what was once a dreary space into a comfortable environment you can't wait to spend time in. That's fantastic progress, so celebrate it! What if you've been finding it hard to declutter? But today, you sorted out one drawer or shelf. That's progress! Celebrate it! It's okay if it's just one drawer. No matter what you do or how you do it, the small victories add up and will add up.

Celebrating progress isn't just about rewards or treats—although they work well too! It's a form of self-care since it reminds you that you're capable and every step you take toward a cleaner, more organized home is worth celebrating.

But what happens when the winds of change blow, and you're asked to adapt to new circumstances? Here, your ability to recognize achievement becomes a powerful tool for embracing change, transforming unfamiliar territory into a new adventure.

ADAPTING TO CHANGES

Life is like a river, constantly flowing and changing its course. To adapt to these changes means to be like water—flexible. For those times when your new habits make it feel like you're thrown into a rapid current, adapting to changes is not about fighting the current but learning how to swim with it.

Life Events and Transitions

Let's not sugar-coat this: the first few weeks of starting a new ADHD-friendly cleaning routine can be hectic. You might wonder, *What's going to change? How will I handle it?* Well, let's break it down so you know what to expect and how to handle it.

- **Shift in your day-to-day life:** You'll be integrating new cleaning habits, so your usual schedule may change. You might be used to chilling out after dinner, but now you'll be doing a quick 10-minute tidy-up. This change is manageable—start off slow, with just 5 minutes of cleaning, and gradually increase it.
- **How you view your home:** You might start seeing your home as a project instead of a living space. In some ways, this can be a double-edged sword since, on the one hand, you'll feel more responsible for your surroundings, while on the other, keeping them up can feel like a burden. Here's a tip: Don't stress about perfection—a home is meant to be lived in, not just looked at.

Adjusting to these changes might not always be smooth sailing. Nevertheless, every life event or transition is also an opportunity for growth. Keep a positive attitude, be patient with yourself, and don't let life events get in the way. But how do you get through these choppy waters? By adjusting your routines.

Adjusting Routines

By adjusting your routines, you *tailor* your daily activities, along with your ADHD symptoms, to suit your needs and lifestyle. It's like customizing your car to suit your taste. Now, why adjust routines at all? Well, life is dynamic, not static. Just as you don't stay the same, your routines shouldn't either—they should evolve with you. Think of it this way: You're not the same person you were five years ago, are you? Your interests, your needs, and your priorities have all changed. This is precisely why your routines might need the occasional re-vamp.

It's perfectly okay to adjust routines. Don't feel guilty or think it means you'll slip up from here on in. Adjusting routines is like tailoring a suit. You want it to fit you just right—not too tight, not too loose. And sometimes, you have to take in or let out a seam here or there to get the perfect fit.

Embracing Flexibility

The need for flexibility arises from the *unique* challenges associated with ADHD. Issues with time management and staying on task can make a rigid cleaning schedule feel like an uphill battle. You might start dusting the living room, only to find yourself organizing the kitchen cabinet half an hour later. This is why flexibility is so critical. Sticking to an ADHD-friendly cleaning schedule means recognizing it's okay not to have a strict schedule. There will be times when you won't be able to do everything you planned, and shifting gears will be necessary.

- If you can't scrub the bathroom on Monday, you can always do it on Tuesday or even Wednesday.
- If you've planned to dust and vacuum on Tuesday, but an unexpected work call pops up. Simply move this chore to a different time slot or even to the next day.
- If you feel more motivated to clean the kitchen instead of the living room, go for it! The key is to work with your energy levels and not against them.

As you adapt your chores to your shifting traits—something your ADHD brain is particularly equipped to enjoy—and just like that, you become a more efficient cleaner and a lifelong learner. The beauty of embracing flexibility in your routine is that it naturally encourages an environment of continual learning—each new approach or technique you try enhances your knowledge and skills.

CONTINUAL LEARNING

Continual learning is your best bet for sticking to an ADHD-friendly cleaning routine, and here's why. First, it keeps your brain engaged. The ADHD brain thrives on novelty and challenges. By constantly learning new strategies and techniques, you're providing your brain with the stimulation it craves to keep your focus sharp.

Second, ongoing learning promotes long-term growth. By doing so, you refine strategies that work best for your unique ADHD traits and discard those that don't. As a result of this trial-and-error process, self-awareness and self-management improve (Sutton, 2016). Other research supports this, too. Continual learning promotes self-efficacy—a belief in your abilities to handle different situations (Nieminen et al., 2019)—a perfect antidote to anxiety around a new routine.

Interestingly, this constant cycle of learning and refining goes beyond maintaining a routine to stay ahead of the game. Just as the world around us is constantly changing, so must our knowledge and skills to deal with it confidently.

Staying Updated

Keeping abreast of ADHD and cleaning strategies is like updating your car's GPS. As cleaning techniques evolve, staying informed enhances your ADHD-friendly cleaning routine. Each new insight is another tool in your housekeeping arsenal, a step toward managing your space and finding tranquility amid clutter. You can stay updated with industry trends through resources like ADDitude and CHADD, both very popular places to find the latest strategies, expert opinions, and real-life experiences. You don't need to adopt every trend; just concentrate on what resonates with you. Listen to your needs, embrace trial and error, and experiment until you find what works best.

Learning is a brain exercise. Each time you explore a new cleaning strategy, you flex your brain muscles, keeping them agile. Over time, you'll make better decisions about what works best for you, tweak your routines, adjust your strategies, and keep things fresh.

Embracing the latest trends in ADHD-friendly cleaning strategies is not only empowering but also makes your day-to-day tasks less stressful—it's nice to know there are others out there going through the same thing. In fact, there's a whole community out there ready to support and guide you.

Engaging With ADHD Communities

There are many ADHD communities filled with people who have been there, done that, and have found solutions. And the best part? They're easily accessible:

- ADHD support community on Reddit
- ADDitude's ADHD forums
- ADHD support groups on Facebook
- ADHD forum on HealthUnlocked

- ADHD community on Psych Central
- CHADD's adult ADHD support forum
- TotallyADD forums

These communities are not just about learning but also about sharing. You can contribute your own insights and experiences, which could potentially help others in the same boat. It's a give-and-take relationship that fosters a sense of belonging and camaraderie. They provide a safe space for you to share your experiences and challenges and, in return, receive emotional support and validation.

But that's not all. By staying engaged with these communities, you get to be part of a continual growth process. ADHD research and understanding is ever evolving, with new strategies continually explored and shared. Ultimately, staying with others within your community keeps you updated and adaptable but also encourages a sense of responsibility toward your own growth. When you're part of a community, there's an added layer of accountability motivating you to stick to your routine. And who knows? You might just find some lifelong friends along the way—people who can push you to step outside your comfort zone and try new approaches. Then, as you exchange experiences, you're inevitably inspired to try out new strategies, enhance your ADHD-friendly cleaning routine, and take your growth journey to the next level.

Experimenting With New Strategies

When you experiment with new cleaning strategies, you flex a crucial aspect of your brain's functionality. This phenomenon is called neuroplasticity.

Neuroplasticity is your brain's amazing ability to adapt and change based on your experiences. Just as you might stumble upon a more efficient way to dust your bookshelves, your brain is constantly adjusting its structure and function in response to new information, experiences, and challenges. Every time you try a new technique or solve a routine problem, you give your brain a workout, encouraging it to form new neural connections and strengthen existing ones.

When you devise a new cleaning strategy—you're reordering your physical space, yes, but at the same time, you're creating a new mental map in your brain. Each decision you make, from the choice of cleaning products to the sequence of tasks, fires up a unique pattern of neural activity. This repeated exercise of decision-making and problem-solving encourages your brain to forge new neural pathways, strengthening its capacity to adapt and evolve (Call, 2019).

In a nutshell, never underestimate the power of seemingly simple actions. They might just be the catalyst for an extraordinary neurological revolution right there in your brain.

A LIFELONG JOURNEY OF MASTERING SPACE

Rob was a lifelong ADHD warrior. His home, much like his mind, never lacked ideas or projects—countless unfinished tasks scattered around the house, each one a testament to his relentless creativity. But this disarray took a toll on Rob's mental health, and he knew something had to change.

He started with a simple long-term strategy: The "10-second rule." Every morning, he'd pick up a few cluttered items around the house and contemplate (in ten seconds) if he *really* needed the item he was holding. Some days, it was as simple as sorting the paperwork. Other times, it was tackling that dreaded junk drawer. The point was that he was making consistent progress, *and* it was manageable. But Rob was realistic. He knew his ADHD could throw a wrench in his plans. So, he found strength in a resource he'd never considered before: the ADHD community. Online support groups became his lifeline. They taught him how to adapt his strategies to new circumstances, how to forgive himself when things slipped, and how to celebrate even the smallest victories. Rob also started consuming educational resources on ADHD. Books, podcasts, TED Talks—he researched everything he could find to better understand his brain and how to work with it.

Today, Rob's house is a testament to his continuous growth. His story is a reminder that with the right strategies, community support, and knowledge, mastering your environment with ADHD is possible.

Key takeaway: When it comes to ADHD and housekeeping, long-term strategies and continual growth are key to maintaining success. In the grand scheme of things, it's the consistent steps that lead to monumental strides, and you're capable of more than you know. But have you ever considered how your external environment impacts ADHD and housekeeping?

9

PRACTICAL CLEANING STRATEGIES TAILORED FOR ADHD

The objective of cleaning is not just to clean, but to feel happiness living within that environment.

— MARIE KONDO

Think of these strategies as methods to encourage focus and reduce distractions. First, we break down your home into manageable "zones"—each room is its own project. Then, we create a custom cleaning routine for each zone. We keep the tasks small and time-bound so you won't lose focus. The beauty of these methods is they're *tailored* to how your brain works. They use your natural energy and focus cycles, so you're not fighting against them. As you work your way through them, feel free to tweak and tailor them to you. That's the beauty of cleaning strategies *tailored* for ADHD.

THE LIVING ROOM RETREAT

Picture this: you, sinking into a clean, soft sofa, surrounded by an orderly, welcoming space. Sounds appealing, right? Now, let's make that happen.

Supplies:

- vacuum cleaner
- microfiber cloths and dusters
- all-purpose cleaner
- glass cleaner
- disinfectant wipes
- furniture polish

Identifying Clutter Hotspots

See your coffee table? It's a prime example of a clutter hotspot—magazines, mail, cups... you name it, it's probably there. Here's a quick fix—use a decorative tray to corral these items. And the entertainment center? It's a magnet for DVDs, video games, and a random assortment of knick-knacks. How about using labeled boxes or baskets to categorize items? Your couch, believe it or not, can be a major hotspot, too. Between cushions, you might find everything from crumbs to loose change. Even floor spaces, especially corners behind furniture, can become clutter hotspots if not regularly checked.

The trick to identifying these zones is to be aware of where items tend to gather. Once you know where the mess accumulates, you can take steps to prevent it, like designated storage spaces, a regular clean-up routine, or adopting a minimalist approach.

Simplifying Decor

Here's a nugget of wisdom: living room decor doesn't have to be overpowering. Start by decluttering. You know, that pile of papers you'll never need again or the knick-knacks collecting dust? Let them go to create a calm and distraction-free environment:

- Adopt the "less is more" philosophy—choose furniture with clean lines and minimal designs to reduce visual noise.
- Consider a minimalist color palette. Too many colors can be visually overstimulating. For a soothing palette—think pastels, neutrals, and cool blues. These hues are known for their calming effects.

- Focus on functionality when it comes to storage. Choose furniture that doubles as storage space. Get creative with it! Consider multipurpose furniture like ottomans with storage space or shelves that hold baskets.

Embrace open spaces and resist the urge to fill every corner of the room. Open spaces give your eyes and mind a break.

Quick Clean Routines

Here's a quick, practical cleaning strategy *tailored* just for you. Before you go, don't forget to gamify your cleaning with setting rewards or challenges. Crank up your favorite tunes or listen to an audiobook to make things feel less like a chore and more like "you" time.

1. Pick up any stray items on the floor, couch, or tables. Set a timer for 5 minutes and pick up as much as you can in that time.
2. Challenge yourself to ditch five things you don't use or need.
3. Grab your trusty dusting cloth and wipe down surfaces. Run it across your coffee table, TV stand, and side tables, and don't forget about your electronics and cables.

4. Your vacuum is your best friend in this battle against dirt. Give the floor a good once-over, and if your couch has removable cushions, vacuum underneath them, too.

One last thing—if you have the space, keep your cleaning supplies in the living room. Use decorative containers or multipurpose storage. This reduces the friction of having to fetch them from another room and keeps you focused.

Storage Hacks for Common Items

Clever storage hacks leverage unused spaces, doubling up furniture functionalities and using containers creatively. Here are some nifty storage hacks to help you keep things sorted.

- **Think vertical:** Shelves, wall-mounted baskets, or hanging organizers keep items off the floor.
- **Use baskets:** Keep one in the corner of your room and put everything that clogs up your spaces into the baskets.
- **Multi-purpose furniture:** Think ottomans that double as storage boxes or coffee tables with built-in shelves.
- **Hooks and hangers:** Hang your coats, scarves, or even headphones on hooks.

- **Drawer organizers:** These are great for small items like keys, pens, and notepads. No more rummaging around in a messy drawer!

The more room you create, the more inviting your living room will be.

THE 5-MINUTE LIVING ROOM TRANSFORMATION

Meet Daryl, a 39-year-old maintenance engineer. Daryl was diagnosed with ADHD in his early 30s and, after much research, finally realized why he could never keep his living room tidy. Everything changed when he discovered he works best in bursts, so he set a five-minute timer and got going. He began with a quick clean routine, picking up everything out of place. Anything that didn't belong in the living room went into a "move it" box. Daryl's always been good at spotting patterns, so he quickly identified his clutter hotspots: the coffee table and the couch. He focused his energy there. After that, Daryl tackled storage. He knew too many choices would overwhelm him, so he opted for simple, large bins. He labeled each one as "bits and bobs," "letters and papers," and "electronics." It's a simple hack, but it helped him know where to put things. Then, he reconsidered his decor. He loves his eclectic knick-knacks, but they're dust magnets and clutter catalysts. So, he chose a few favorites and stored the rest.

When the timer rang, Daryl looked around—his living room was transformed. It's not perfect, but it's his, and it's a lot more manageable now.

THE KITCHEN CONQUEST

Picture yourself in a spotless, organized kitchen—the sizzle of a pan, the aroma of fresh herbs, and finding every tool you need right at your fingertips. Here's a list of what you'll need:

- all-purpose cleaner
- degreaser
- scrub brushes and sponges
- microfiber cloths
- disinfectant
- baking soda and vinegar
- trash bags
- dish soap

Counter and Sink Strategies

First, let's tackle the counter. They're always a catch-all for all sorts of things. To curb this, assign a specific place for everything. But only for the items you absolutely need—fewer items mean less clutter to distract you.

- Designate specific spots for frequently used items like your coffee maker or toaster. This way, they have a "home" to return to.
- Use containers or trays to group similar items together.

Next, the sink.

- Start by breaking it down. Instead of tackling a mountain of dishes, wash them as you go.
- Done with a cup or plate? Make it a rule to never leave dishes in the sink—rinse and load them into the dishwasher right away. If you don't have a dishwasher, designate a dishwashing time each day.

If you're struggling to get started, turn it into a game. Set a timer for 15 minutes and see how much you can get done before it goes off.

To stay on top of the counter and sink, do a quick clean-up every evening—a simple wipe down and wash up can work wonders.

ADHD-Friendly Pantry and Fridge Organization

You never know the true value of organization until you're paralyzed by an ADHD-induced whirlwind. You don't need to achieve Pinterest-perfect pantries and fridges; it's more about making your life simpler and less stressful.

- **Start with decluttering:** Excess items lead to sensory overload, so purge! Toss out expired products, donate unneeded items, and you'll already be halfway there.
- **Categorize:** Group similar items together. Grains with grains, canned goods with canned goods, snacks with snacks—you get the idea. For the fridge, dairy in one section, veggies in another, and condiments in the door compartments. You need to create a logical flow that makes sense to you.
- **Clear storage containers:** ADHD often comes with an "out of sight, out of mind" phenomenon. To counter this, use clear storage containers for your pantry items, and for your fridge, consider tiered shelves or turntables, too.
- **Labeling:** Label everything. It's your secret weapon against forgetfulness. Whether it's a shelf for dairy or a container for leftovers,

keep it simple, and don't worry about fancy tags; a simple masking tape with a marker will do.

Once you've found a system that works, stick to it. Spend a few minutes each day to tidy up—regular upkeep prevents things from spiraling out of control.

Streamlining Meal Prep and Clean-Up

With a little planning and some smart strategies, you can whip up a storm in the kitchen without the aftermath looking like one. As always, practice makes perfect, so don't be disheartened if it takes a few tries to get it right.

- **Organize:** Categorizing your utensils and ingredients in specific areas is a great way to speed up your cooking process while making clean-up easier.
- Organize your kitchen in zones—a prepping area, a cooking area, and a cleaning area.
- Another pro tip is to use multi-purpose tools. A vegetable chopper that chops, peels, and slices or a pot that sautés, boils, and bakes is worth its weight in gold.
- **Have a plan:** Menus aren't just for fancy restaurants—having a weekly or even a

monthly menu helps you shop efficiently and waste less.
- Choose simple recipes with fewer ingredients.
- Pre-cut veggies and pre-cooked proteins are a lifesaver in cutting down prep time.
- **Batch cooking:** Take advantage of your hyperfocus phases, cook in large quantities, and then freeze portions for later. All you'll need to do is cook one day, have meals ready for the entire week, and have less washing up to do.

To tackle the clean-up, "clean as you go" is a mantra you should live by. Rinse off dishes as soon as you're done using them, and it will save you a mountain of work later.

A SWITCH FROM A CHAOTIC KITCHEN TO A CULINARY HAVEN

Meet Jin, a 41-year-old culinary enthusiast with ADHD. Jin's ADHD symptoms limited Jin's creativity and passion for cooking—the kitchen was a mess. But this narrative is about Jin's transformation from a chaotic kitchen to a culinary haven using ADHD-friendly strategies.

Starting with counter and sink strategies, Jin adopted the "clean as you go" approach. This meant washing dishes immediately after using them, wiping down counters, and putting ingredients away as soon as he was done. Next, Jin reorganized his pantry and fridge in a way that made sense to his ADHD brain. To decrease the time he spent searching for ingredients and reduce his frustration, he grouped similar items together and used clear containers to see what he had. He then streamlined his meal prep and clean-up process. Jin began planning his meals ahead of time, prepping ingredients in advance, and using fewer utensils. At the end of his prep, he tackled his dish problem. Instead of letting them pile up, Jin set a timer for 15 minutes each day dedicated to washing dishes, wiping down surfaces, and reorganizing his cupboards. Today, Jin's kitchen is a reflection of his passion for food—organized, functional, and a joy to cook in.

THE BATHROOM BATTLE

The bathroom battle is one real-life saga we all face. But it doesn't have to be. It's manageable as long as you have the right supplies and a routine.

Supplies:

- cleaning gloves
- mop and bucket
- bathroom cleaner

- microfiber cloths
- toilet cleaner
- glass cleaner
- squeegee

Quick Daily Routine to Prevent Build-up

When you clean regularly, you tackle small messes before they become big problems. Plus, it's easier to maintain a fresh, clean bathroom than to scrub a heavily soiled one. Here's your quick-hit guide to keep things orderly without eating up your day.

1. **Set a timer:** Give yourself 20 minutes each day for bathroom tidying. It's amazing what you can achieve in so little time!
2. **Sink:** Most bathrooms are centered around their sinks. Wipe it down with a cloth dampened with a mild cleaner. Don't forget the faucet and knobs!
3. **Toilet:** Spray the toilet bowl with cleaner and let it sit while you clean the rest of the bathroom. Wipe the seat and handle with disinfecting wipes.
4. **Mirror and counter:** Use a glass cleaner on your mirror and wipe it down. Clear the counter of clutter and give it a good wipe.

5. **Shower and tub:** A quick spray with a daily shower cleaner can prevent soap scum build-up. No scrubbing necessary!
6. **Floors and mats:** Give the floor a quick sweep and shake out any rugs or mats.
7. **Finally, the toilet bowl:** Grab your toilet brush, scrub the bowl, and then flush.

And there you have it—just a few minutes a day can keep your bathroom looking fresh and clean. To take your cleaning and organizing to the next level, let's look into those specific parts of your bathroom that need a bit more attention.

Keeping Surfaces Clear

Clutter-free bathrooms can absolutely be a sanctuary, and keeping surfaces clear is a critical part of achieving that serenity. Let's dive into some practical strategies:

1. Begin with the sink and work your way around the bathroom, picking up any items that aren't in their designated spot. Don't get sidetracked with organizing; just put everything in a basket for now.
2. Next, grab your cleaning supplies—spray all the surfaces and wipe them down.

3. Keep your cleaning supplies in the bathroom. This way, you don't need to go hunting for them when it's time to clean.
4. After a quick wipe-down, take a look at the items in your basket. Decide what you need and what you don't. Try to resist the urge to place items back on the surfaces—the goal is to keep them clear.
5. Discard any empty bottles or expired products. The fewer items you have, the less cluttered your bathroom will be.
6. Designate a home for each item you decide to keep. Consider using drawer organizers or storage bins.

To make decluttering a daily habit, set a timer for just 5 minutes a day. In this short burst of time, target one surface in your bathroom. It could be your sink, your shower, or your bathroom cabinets.

Organizing Toiletries

The chaos of toiletries—fancy lotions battling half-empty shampoo bottles and rogue toothpaste tubes oozing onto the countertop. They may seem innocent individually, but together they form an unruly army, complicating your morning routine instead of streamlining it. Here's how to organize them:

- **Declutter:** Get rid of anything unnecessary or expired—every item not serving a purpose is just taking up space.
- **Sort by use:** Everyday essentials like toothpaste, soap, and shampoo should be easily accessible, while you can store away rarely used items.
- **Clear containers:** This way, you can instantly see what's inside without rummaging around. It's also satisfying to see everything neatly arranged!
- **Limit bulk purchases:** Bulk purchases create clutter, so only buy what you'll use within a certain time frame.
- **Regular decluttering:** Set aside a few minutes each week to check your toiletries—put items back in their designated spots after each use.

Combatting Common Mess Culprits

Here are a few strategies to combat everyday causes of mess in the bathroom:

- **Hair:** A notorious culprit. Instead of letting hair clog your drain, use a drain cover to catch loose strands. After showering, remove the cover, toss the hair in the bin, and voila! Regular sweeping or vacuuming will also help.

- **Toothpaste:** To remove those sticky blobs on your sink, faucet, and mirror, dampen a microfiber cloth with warm water and wipe them away. Make it a habit to clean up right after brushing.
- **Soap scum:** A squeegee is a game-changer. After showering, swipe it over your tiles and glass to prevent buildup. Pair it with a weekly scrub using a vinegar and water solution.
- **Water spots:** Common on mirrors and faucets. Wipe down these areas after use to prevent build-up. For tough spots, warm water with a splash of vinegar works wonders.

Consistency is key. Small, regular clean-ups greatly reduce the mess and help keep your bathroom spick and span.

CASE STUDY: THE MAGIC OF ROUTINE IN MAINTAINING A SPARKLING BATHROOM

Meet Tara, a software engineer in her mid-thirties diagnosed with ADHD in her early teens. As an adult, she learned to leverage her traits to excel in her profession. Keeping her bathroom tidy was another matter. This case study explores how Tara discovered the magic of routine to conquer this challenge.

The turning point came when Tara learned about ADHD-friendly cleaning strategies. She started by identifying common mess culprits like wet towels and toothpaste spills. By hanging a towel rack on the back of the door and keeping a washcloth handy, she tackled these issues head-on. Next, she focused on keeping surfaces clear. Tara realized clutter was a major distraction, so she made a rule: "If it's not in use, it's not on the counter." This simple mantra made a big difference to the overall feel of the bathroom. Her next move was to organize toiletries logically. "I used labeled baskets to group similar items together and kept only what I used on the surfaces. I spent way less time searching for things organizing the bathroom like this!" But the real magic came with a quick daily routine—"wiping down surfaces five minutes each day was manageable and didn't feel overwhelming." Tara's bathroom is now a sparkling sanctuary, and her story illustrates the power of routine.

Key takeaway: With ADHD-friendly methods, you'll learn how to keep things clean in a bathroom, even if it's difficult at first. What's more, mastering high-traffic areas is just the start; imagine the ripple effect it'll have on the entire house. Now, let's reflect on how a tidy living space improves your quality of life.

THE DEEPER MEANING OF A TIDY HOME

What does a tidy home really feel like? Yes, it's clean and clutter-free, but it's much more than that. Keeping your surroundings tidy is like orchestrating a symphony of harmony and balance. Each tidy corner is a note in the symphony, contributing to the tone. And when your home resonates with tranquility like this, your mind follows suit.

BEYOND THE PHYSICAL

Beyond the physical relates to the emotions, thoughts, and energy we can't physically touch. A clean house is nice, but there is more to it than that. When you walk into a clutter-free space, you don't just see the order;

you *feel* it. In the same way that sound waves travel through the air and light waves reach your eyes, the energy of a space has real effects. It's not something you can measure with a ruler or see with a microscope, but it's there—like the hum of background noise. It's a subtle undercurrent influencing how we perceive our surroundings, how we interact with others, and, ultimately, how we feel about ourselves. It's an unseen, intangible element, but it's as real as the air we breathe.

Mental Clarity and Emotional Stability From Cleanliness

The same is true for clean, organized environments, where physical cleanliness enhances your mental and emotional well-being. Mental clarity means having a clear mind—when your thoughts are organized and you focus without distractions. On the other hand, clutter is distracting—it pulls your attention in all directions, reducing your concentration and causing stress. When you clear out the clutter, you create physical and mental space. Suddenly, there's room for new ideas, fresh thoughts, and creativity. Emotional stability and mood are strongly influenced by your environment, too. Ever notice how a messy room makes you feel anxious or overwhelmed? That's because clutter is a visual representation of life's chaotic aspects. It reminds you of tasks unfinished, causing guilt or stress.

Conversely, a clean environment is calming—it promotes feelings of accomplishment, control, and satisfaction.

But why should you care?

- Your mental health is as important as your physical health. And just like how a balanced diet and regular exercise contribute to physical wellness, a clean environment does wonders for your mental well-being.
- When your space is clean, you're more likely to invite people over. Social interaction improves your mood and reduces loneliness.
- A clean space also has a positive effect on your sleep, which is vital for both physical and mental health.
- Even better are the therapeutic benefits of cleaning. It's a mindful activity that keeps you in the present moment, reducing stress and anxiety.
- And let's not forget the satisfaction you get when you see the results of your hard work.

Spaces That Inspire

The deeper meaning of a tidy home doesn't stop at your well-being. You might think inspiration is something that just hits you out of the blue. But did you know your environment can be a huge source of motivation and creativity? Architect and design expert Donald Rattner asserts design elements like lighting, color, and layout greatly affect mood and inspiration levels (Ratner, 2023). But how do you create such a conducive environment?

- Other than organization and cleanliness, take advantage of natural elements like sunlight and plants to elevate mood and receive 6% more productivity and 15% more creativity at home (Ford, 2017).
- Bright colors like yellow and orange stimulate creativity, while cooler tones induce calm. Decorations tailored to reflect personal interests and tastes also keep motivation high (Ferguson, 2020).
- Designate specific spaces for different activities to promote productivity.
- Balance functionality and aesthetics with smart storage and aesthetically pleasing furniture to boost clear thinking and idea generation.

So, if you're looking for inspiration, take a look around. Is your home supporting your creativity or inhibiting it? Is it time to declutter, clean, and maybe even redecorate? After all, your environment is more than just a backdrop to your life; it's a source of inspiration and a catalyst for creativity.

PERSONAL GROWTH AND ADHD

Personal growth goes beyond the big things, like landing your dream job or running a marathon. It also relates to the small, everyday actions that reflect our inner changes. The act of tidying up is symbolic of your personal growth. It signifies your journey from chaos to order, from indecision to clarity, and from the past to the present.

Evolving Self-Concepts

A self-concept is the mental image of who we are. It shapes our behavior and decisions. When you're struggling with routine tasks, it's easy to develop a negative self-concept. You might start believing you're incapable or inadequate, which isn't true at all.

Now, what's this got to do with a tidy home? Well, everything. Tidying up is an exercise in self-management, a way to assert control over your surroundings. When you successfully maintain a clean home, it directly challenges negative beliefs. Each completed task, be it washing dishes or sweeping floors, is a small victory boosting your self-esteem. And because your home is an extension of your self-concept, the way you maintain your home reflects and influences how you see yourself.

The deeper meaning of a tidy home comes down to this:

- It's a form of self-care and self-expression.
- It's a way of nurturing your self-concept, of telling yourself, "I can do this. I am capable. I value my environment and myself."

So, when you look at your tidy home, understand it's a testament to your ability to overcome challenges, manage your ADHD, and improve your self-concept. In essence, it's a tangible representation of your resilience and strength. Let's take a closer look at some of the challenges you've overcome or are about to overcome to improve your self-concept.

Overcoming Challenges

Achieving success despite obstacles requires resilience, patience, and determination. As you work your way through these ADHD-friendly strategies, you've overcome many challenges, and you should be proud of yourself.

- **Distraction:** Remember how your attention used to dart from one task to another, leaving multiple cleaning jobs half-done? You've learned to beat this by breaking tasks into smaller, manageable parts. Now, you systematically focus on one room or even just one corner at a time and finish one job before moving on to the next.
- **Procrastination:** There was a time when ADHD made you put off tasks that felt overwhelming. But you didn't let that get the better of you. Instead of avoiding cleaning altogether, you began to set a timer for short bursts of activity. Even fifteen minutes, you found, could make a big difference.
- **Impulsivity:** You might recall how you used to start a major decluttering project on a whim, only to lose interest halfway through. By planning before starting, you have successfully counteracted this. Now, you list the tasks you need to accomplish and stick to it.
- **Time management:** ADHD made it difficult for you to estimate how long tasks would take. By scheduling and timing your cleaning tasks with a planner or app, you now stay on track and get a little motivation boost by seeing your progress.

- **Lack of motivation:** Cleaning once felt like a chore and bored you. But you've innovated to turn it into a game or include some fun elements like music or podcasts. Now, you keep yourself entertained, turning cleaning into a fun activity instead of a chore.

Never forget that you're developing vital skills that extend far beyond the immediate challenge of routine and tidying up. So, next time you feel like you can't get started or will never finish, remember—this isn't a problem; it's an opportunity for growth.

Recognizing the Journey

Our lives are shaped by each step we take, each decision we make, every success we achieve, and every failure we experience. In other words, recognizing the journey means taking stock of your accomplishments and appreciating your challenges. By acknowledging the journey, we can reflect on our experiences, learn from them, and apply these insights to the future. In the end, your ADHD-cleaning journey isn't just about maintaining a tidy home—it's a profound journey of:

- Self-acceptance by accepting yourself, flaws and all, and realizing your struggles with tidiness do not define your worth.

- Self-discovery by helping you understand your strengths, weaknesses, and the unique ways your ADHD brain works.
- Personal growth by teaching you discipline, patience, and the importance of creating a serene space for yourself.

This journey is an adventure waiting to unfold, and you've got everything you need to make it an incredible one. So, embrace it wholeheartedly, and you'll learn how to create a more organized living space but also a deeper connection with yourself.

THE BROADER IMPACT

A tidy home is not just about personal benefits. It has a more profound impact extending far beyond the individual level. Here's how:

- reduces anxiety and stress and promotes mental health
- enhances productivity and creativity by reducing distractions
- controls the spread of germs and diseases, contributing to health
- encourages a culture of care and responsibility for you and your family

- enhances interpersonal relationships
- reflects respect for your possessions

Positive Influence on Others

When you maintain a clean and organized home, it creates an atmosphere of discipline and orderliness, something that can rub off on your guests or anyone who visits. The neat environment communicates your values of cleanliness, care, and respect for personal space. As a result, those who visit you might feel inspired to adopt similar habits in their own homes. Imagine being a positive influence without even uttering a word!

What's more, a clean home is a reflection of a healthy lifestyle. It sends out a message that you prioritize health and well-being, which could inspire others to do the same. In essence, your tidy home serves as a silent yet potent motivator for yourself and others to embrace cleanliness and organization.

A Haven for Self and Family

A clean, organized space sends a message of relaxation. It whispers, "Welcome home, you can unwind now." Think about your favorite room. Is it clean and tidy? Clean spaces are inviting and boost our mood. They make us want to spend time there, sharing moments with family or simply enjoying our own company. A clean home is also good for our physical health. It minimizes allergens like dust and mold that trigger allergies and respiratory problems. The simple act of cleaning is also a great workout! Sweeping, mopping, and dusting burn almost 160 calories, while more heavy-duty chores can burn up to 350 calories (Cronkleton, 2022). It's a win-win!

Finally, a clean home is a great environment for kids. It encourages discipline, responsibility, and focus by showing them the importance of taking care of their surroundings and sets a positive example.

So go ahead. Dust off that shelf, sweep that floor, and declutter that drawer. You're creating a safe haven—one that shelters, comforts, and rejuvenates. A haven that's yours.

The Ripple Effect in Other Life Areas

Here's something interesting: The habit of keeping your home clean and organized has ripple effects throughout your life. It's all about discipline and consistency, two traits that are crucial for success in any endeavor. For example, following a routine requires planning and regular effort. These habits translate into better time management skills, improved work efficiency, and even financial discipline. Other ways you'll affect your life include:

- better sleep
- healthy eating
- saves money
- teaches responsibility
- helps in time management

Additionally, a clean and organized home is like a constant reminder of your ability to maintain order and control in your life. This increased self-esteem could motivate you to tackle other challenges with a positive mindset.

In conclusion, a tidy home is a tool, a catalyst for personal growth, and a medium to inspire others. So, the next time you tackle the dusty blinds or arrange your shelves, tell yourself that you're doing much more than cleaning; you're shaping lives, starting with your own.

FINDING INNER PEACE THROUGH CLEANING

Meet George, a 22-year-old graduate. Diagnosed with ADHD in his early teens, he struggled to control the turbulence of his thoughts. But everything changed when he discovered the therapeutic power of a cleaning routine.

ADHD made it difficult for George to focus, causing frequent bouts of anxiety. "Thoughts bounced around my head like a pinball machine," he says. Yet the unpredictable nature of his mind led him to look for peace in unconventional ways. One day, George stumbled upon an article about the calming influence of cleaning. He was never much of a cleaner, but intrigued, he decided to give it a go. He started small—just his desk. He arranged his stationery, wiped down the surface, and threw away unnecessary clutter.

By cleaning, he gained control, creating a pocket of calm in his otherwise chaotic mind. "It was as if, while cleaning, my thoughts, too, fell into place." After this, he extended his cleaning routine to other areas of the home. Upon returning home from university, he used his parent's house as a way to meditate and cope with a cleaning routine. His newly formed habits became an outlet for his hyperactivity and a tool for focus. The more he cleaned, the more he found a rhythm in the mundane, a harmony in the routine, and most importantly, tranquility in the process. This isn't to say that George's ADHD disappeared. "It just made things easy to manage. It was like I finally found a method of self-care unique for me."

So, here's what you need to know. Inner peace might just be a cleaning routine away, even if you're battling something as challenging as ADHD.

Key takeaway: The journey you've taken with ADHD-friendly strategies and the implications they've had on your life merits a moment of reflection. In retrospect, you've learned, unlearned, and relearned several aspects of cleaning. The methods you use today are not just for the present but also for the future, where your strategies are sustainable, inclusive, and adaptive to the ever-changing ADHD landscape.

Pass It On!

Once you have your new strategies in place and you see them working for you, you will feel a greater sense of calm in your home environment … and that will have a ripple effect on the rest of your life. Help someone else find the same transformation.

Simply by sharing your honest opinion of this book and a little about your own experience, you'll show new readers where they can find all the strategies they need to make their ADHD into a cleaning asset.

IN UNDER 1 MINUTE
YOU CAN HELP OTHERS JUST LIKE YOU BY LEAVING A REVIEW!

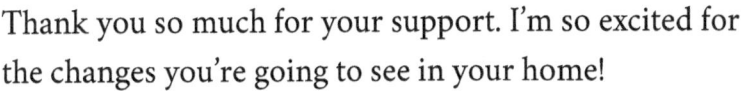

Thank you so much for your support. I'm so excited for the changes you're going to see in your home!

CONCLUSION: EMBRACING THE JOURNEY

During our exploration of ADHD-friendly cleaning strategies, we found methods and practices that were both effective and respectful of the ADHS brain's *unique* neurodiversity. As a result, we have learned that cleaning does not have to be a monotonous task but rather an engaging and rewarding one. Whenever we embark on a journey, it's not with the destination in mind—the journey is transformative in itself. This is especially true for those of us navigating life with ADHD. Understanding your unique mind and how it processes information is the first step toward this new direction.

ADHD is often seen as a barrier, but it can also be a catalyst for creative problem-solving. By understanding how your brain works, you'll develop cleaning strategies *tailored* to your needs. The key here is to take a proactive approach. Understanding alone won't make your home tidy but applying that understanding through action will. It's a continuous process, a series of consistent steps, no matter how small, toward maintaining a clean and serene home.

THE LIFELONG NATURE OF GROWTH AND ADAPTATION

Throughout our lives, we grow, learn, and adapt. This is a universal truth, and it's especially relevant for people with ADHD. Cleaning strategies that work for you now may not work in the future. As we grow, our needs, preferences, and circumstances change. We must adjust our strategies accordingly in order to adapt. This demands flexibility, a willingness to experiment, and the courage to fail and learn. So, don't be disheartened if a strategy stops working. It's not a failure but a sign that you're growing. A change in strategy gives you the chance to learn something new, to adapt, and to find one that's more suitable for you at this point in time.

INSPIRING CHANGE BY SHARING YOUR JOURNEY

You're not alone on this journey. Countless others are seeking a clean, ADHD-friendly home as well. Sharing your journey, your successes, and even your failures can inspire others. It shows them that they, too, can transform their homes and lives through understanding and action. So, don't hesitate to share your journey, your unique strategies, and your insights. In doing so, you both inspire and learn from others. It's a beautiful symbiosis, a community dedicated to growth, adaptation, and the pursuit of tranquil, orderly living.

Final Thoughts: The Beautiful Marriage of ADHD and a Blissful Home

Looking forward, ADHD doesn't have to stand in the way of having a clean, organized home—it can be a catalyst for creative, personalized cleaning strategies. You can transform your home and your life if you understand how your mind works and apply that understanding through habit and routine.

With ADHD-friendly strategies, you're not fighting against your natural tendencies; you're working with them. Your brain operates differently, and that's okay. You can turn what some may see as a weakness into a strength by celebrating and utilizing these differences.

Embrace the whirl of ideas, then learn how to channel them into a cleaning strategy that works for you. Maybe you need color-coded bins, or perhaps you thrive with a visual checklist—there is no one-size-fits-all. What makes a happy home is what suits you, makes you feel comfortable, and keeps your home blissful.

Instead of striving for perfection, embrace the journey and the progress. Enjoy the process, the learning, the growth, and the tranquility of an organized, clean environment. In the end, creating a blissful home serves as a sanctuary for your vibrant, creative, and sometimes scattered mind. So, here's to you: the beautiful marriage of ADHD and a blissful home. It's a journey worth embracing and one you're absolutely capable of mastering.

BONUS CHECKLIST: ADHD-FRIENDLY CLEANING CHECKLIST: WEEK-BY-WEEK

This checklist is your ultimate guide to a clutter-free, clean, and serene living space. Designed exclusively for ADHD brains like yours, this method breaks down the intimidating challenge of cleaning into achievable, bite-sized steps. Each week, you'll focus on a specific area of your home—decluttering, sorting zones of importance, building an easy routine, and the quest for long-term success.

What's unique about this approach? It's designed to work *with* your ADHD. This checklist is visual and engaging and rewards progress. Most of all, it's doable because you'll stay on track without feeling overwhelmed. With it, you're creating a space that supports your mental and emotional health. So, are you ready to transform your home, one week at a time?

Week 1: Setting Up and Decluttering

Day 1: Learn about ADHD traits and reflect on how they influence your cleaning habits. Can hyperfocus make you a cleaning whiz? Does impulsivity cause clutter? Do you get easily distracted?

Day 2: Identify and list down clutter hotspots in high-traffic areas: living room, kitchen, bathroom.

Day 3: Start with the living room—but just the surfaces for now. This includes coffee tables, entertainment centers, bookshelves—any flat surface that attracts clutter.

Day 4: Move to the kitchen. The countertop and sink area are the primary targets. Clear out any dishes, gadgets, or miscellaneous items.

Day 5: Address the bathroom. Organize your toiletries and clear out any unnecessary items from the surfaces. This includes expired products, empty bottles, or items you no longer use.

Day 6: After a busy few days of decluttering, it's time to reflect. How did the routine make you feel? Are there areas that still feel overwhelming? This is not a time for judgment; it's a chance to learn and adjust your approach accordingly.

Day 7: You've worked hard all week, and it's time for a well-deserved break. Relax, reward yourself. Maybe catch up on your favorite podcast or watch a movie. This rest time rewards all you've done so far and helps you recharge for the week ahead.

Week 2: Organizing and Zone Cleaning

Day 1: Familiarize yourself with the concept of zones in your home. Differentiating between high-traffic areas, like the kitchen and living room, and less frequented ones to better understand where clutter accumulates and where to concentrate your cleaning efforts.

Day 2: Once you've identified your home's zones, implement a rotation cleaning system. Using this method, you'll switch between zones regularly, ensuring all areas receive equal attention.

Day 3: Focus on the living room, making it calming and organized. Look into storage solutions for clutter-prone spaces and consider simplifying decor.

Day 4: Transform your kitchen into a streamlined and efficient space. Establish designated zones for preparation, cooking, and cleaning, and arrange items in order of use.

Day 5: Organize your bathroom storage, giving priority to daily-use items. Ensure these items are easily accessible while less frequently used items are stored out of the way.

Day 6: Take a moment to reflect on your organizing process so far. Make adjustments as needed to ensure the system works well for you.

Day 7: Reward yourself with a well-deserved break. Start that new book, sleep in, or dive into a hobby to relax and rejuvenate.

Week 3: Building Habits and Routines

Day 1: Learn about the importance of consistent habits and routines for managing ADHD. Think of resources like TED Talks, podcasts, CHADD, and this book!

Day 2: Kick-start a simple morning routine—put your clothes away, wipe down kitchen surfaces, or anything else you're comfortable with.

Day 3: Implement an evening routine to involve tidying the living room and preparing the kitchen for breakfast the next day.

Day 4: Midweek check: How are the routines holding? Adjust based on how you're feeling and the progress (or not) you've made so far. Make tweaks as necessary to ensure your routines serve a purpose.

Day 5: Incorporate a quick bathroom wipe-down into either your morning or evening routine.

Day 6: Reflect on how these routines are impacting your life. Do they make you feel more in control and less overwhelmed? Use these feelings to motivate you going forward.

Day 7: Reward yourself on the day of rest. Get a takeout, have a movie marathon, or any other treat as a way to celebrate your hard work and dedication.

Week 4: Refinement and Long-Term Vision

Day 1: Reflect on your progress over the past three weeks. Identify what strategies worked well and what aspects felt challenging to better understand your cleaning and organizing habits.

Day 2: Based on your reflections, adjust and refine your strategies to better suit your needs and preferences. You want to create a system that works for you.

Day 3: Schedule monthly check-ins on your calendar to revisit and refine your routines. This will help keep you on track and allow for necessary adjustments.

Day 4: Create a visible reminder of your zones and cleaning rotations. Placing it somewhere prominent will serve as a constant reminder of your goals.

Day 5: Set up a reward system—treat yourself to something special to boost your motivation and keep up with your routines.

Day 6: Connect with an online ADHD community. Sharing experiences and gaining insights from others facing similar challenges provide additional strategies and encouragement.

Day 7: Celebrate a month of transformation! Reflect on the deeper meaning of your tidy space, like how it contributes to your well-being, productivity, and overall quality of life.

REFERENCES

Aliouche, H. (2022, January 18). *Investigating the link between cleaning and mental health.* News-Medical.net. https://www.news-medical.net/health/Investigating-the-Link-between-Cleaning-and-Mental-Health.aspx#:

Baobaid, S. (2017, July 10). *Finding inspiration in your surroundings.* Youth Time Magazine. https://youthtimemag.com/where-is-inspiration-look-around-you/#:

Barzacchini, M. (2022, March 29). *How to be an accountability partner.* Mind Tools. https://www.mindtools.com/blog/how-to-be-an-accountability-partner-mttalk-roundup/

Belsky, G. (2019, August 5). *ADHD and messiness.* Understood. https://www.understood.org/en/articles/adhd-and-messiness-what-you-need-to-know

Bertin, M. (2017, November 3). *The effects of ADHD on communication.* ADD Resource Center. https://www.addrc.org/effects-adhd-communication/

Bettino, K. (2021, May 24). *9 tips for creating a routine for adults with ADHD.* Psych Central. https://psychcentral.com/adhd/9-tips-for-creating-a-routine-for-adults-with-adhd#:

Bhanji, J. P., & Delgado, M. R. (2013, October 8). The social brain and reward: Social information processing in the human striatum. *Wiley Interdisciplinary Reviews: Cognitive Science, 5*(1), 61–73. https://doi.org/10.1002/wcs.1266

Blain, T. (2022, October 20). *Habit stacking for ADHD.* Verywell Mind. https://www.verywellmind.com/habit-stacking-definition-steps-benefits-for-adhd-6751145

Blanchfield, T. (2022, May 31). *Types of therapy for ADHD.* Verywell Mind. https://www.verywellmind.com/types-of-therapy-for-adhd-5272434

Blum, K., Chen, A. L.-C., Braverman, E. R., Comings, D. E., Chen, T. J.,

Arcuri, V., Blum, S. H., Downs, B. W., Waite, R. L., Notaro, A., Lubar, J., Williams, L., Prihoda, T. J., Palomo, T., & Oscar-Berman, M. (2008, October). Attention-deficit-hyperactivity disorder and reward deficiency syndrome. *Neuropsychiatric Disease and Treatment, 4*(5), 893–918. https://www.ncbi.nlm.nih.gov/pmc/articles/PMC2626918/

Brennan, D. (2021, October 25). *Psychological benefits of routines*. WebMD. https://www.webmd.com/mental-health/psychological-benefits-of-routine

Call, M. (2019, August 8). *Neuroplasticity: How to use your brain's malleability to improve your well-being*. Accelerate.uofuhealth.utah.edu. https://accelerate.uofuhealth.utah.edu/resilience/neuroplasticity-how-to-use-your-brain-s-malleability-to-improve-your-well-being

Canela, C., Buadze, A., Dube, A., Eich, D., & Liebrenz, M. (2017, September 27). Skills and compensation strategies in adult ADHD – A qualitative study. *PLOS ONE, 12*(9), e0184964. https://doi.org/10.1371/journal.pone.0184964

CHADD. (2018a). *About ADHD - Symptoms, causes and treatment - CHADD*. CHADD. https://chadd.org/about-adhd/overview/

CHADD. (2018b). *Coaching - CHADD*. CHADD. https://chadd.org/about-adhd/coaching/

Cherry, K. (2019, December 10). *How listening to music can have psychological benefits*. Verywell Mind. https://www.verywellmind.com/surprising-psychological-benefits-of-music-4126866

Chirico, A., Serino, S., Cipresso, P., Gaggioli, A., & Riva, G. (2015, June 30). When music "flows". State and trait in musical performance, composition and listening: A systematic review. *Frontiers in Psychology, 6*. https://doi.org/10.3389/fpsyg.2015.00906

Chowdhury, M. R. (2019, April 9). *The neuroscience of gratitude and how it affects anxiety & grief*. PositivePsychology.com. https://positivepsychology.com/neuroscience-of-gratitude/

Clear, J. (2018). *Atomic Habits*. PenguinRandomHouse.

Conner, A. (2022, February 21). *Sense of self: How being misunderstood*

impacts ADHD brains. Www.additudemag.com. https://www.addi
tudemag.com/sense-of-self-being-misunderstood-adhd/#:

Contributors, W. E. (2021, November 25). *Mental health benefits of decluttering*. WebMD. https://www.webmd.com/mental-health/mental-health-benefits-of-decluttering#:

Creative Safety Supply. (2019). *What is 5s? Training for 5s lean methodology, systems & principles*. Creative Safety Supply. https://www.creativesafetysupply.com/content/education-research/5S/index.html

Cridland, J. (2022, March 10). *How many podcasts are there?* Podnews.net. https://podnews.net/article/how-many-podcasts

Cronkleton, E. (2022, April 27). *How many calories Are burned vacuuming and doing housework?* Healthline. https://www.healthline.com/health/fitness/calories-burned-vacuuming#:

Diane Ackerman Quote. (n.d.). A-Z Quotes. https://www.azquotes.com/quote/526125

Doyle, N. (2019, October 30). *Richard Branson opens door to bigger thinking on neurodiversity*. Forbes. https://www.forbes.com/sites/drnancydoyle/2019/10/22/richard-branson-opens-the-door-to-bigger-thinking-on-neurodiversity-/

Drake, K. (2021, September 1). *Adapting the Pomodoro technique for your work style*. Psych Central. https://psychcentral.com/adhd/how-to-adapt-the-pomodoro-technique-adhd

Duhigg, C. (2011). *How habits work*. Charles Duhigg. https://charlesduhigg.com/how-habits-work/

Dutton, J. (2007, March 20). *How swimming saved Michael Phelps: An ADHD story*. ADDitude. https://www.additudemag.com/michael-phelps-adhd-advice-from-the-olympians-mom/

Edgelow, M. (2022, March 18). *What you do every day matters: The power of routines*. Queen's Gazette | Queen's University. https://www.queensu.ca/gazette/stories/what-you-do-every-day-matters-power-routines#:

Edwards, V. (2019, July 29). *The benefits of music: How the science of music can help you*. Science of People. https://www.scienceofpeople.com/benefits-music/#:

Fabiny, A. (2015, February 14). *Music can boost memory and mood - Harvard Health*. Harvard Health. https://www.health.harvard.edu/mind-and-mood/music-can-boost-memory-and-mood

Ferguson, A. L. (2020, January 5). *Five reasons why decorating is good for you: Why you should decorate*. Follow the Yellow Brick Home. https://followtheyellowbrickhome.com/five-reasons-why-home-decorating-is-good-for-you/#:

Ford, B. (2017, May 24). *Harnessing the power of natural light*. Work Design Magazine. https://www.workdesign.com/2017/05/harnessing-power-natural-light/#:

Gardner, B., Lally, P., & Wardle, J. (2012). Making health habitual: The psychology of "habit-formation" and general practice. *British Journal of General Practice, 62*(605), 664–666. https://doi.org/10.3399/bjgp12x659466

Gaspar, J. M., Christie, G. J., Prime, D. J., Jolicœur, P., & McDonald, J. J. (2016, February 22). Inability to suppress salient distractors predicts low visual working memory capacity. *Proceedings of the National Academy of Sciences, 113*(13), 3693–3698. https://doi.org/10.1073/pnas.1523471113

Gawrilow, C., Merkt, J., Goossens–Merkt, H., Bodenburg, S., & Wendt, M. (2011, April 2). Multitasking in adults with ADHD. *ADHD Attention Deficit and Hyperactivity Disorders, 3*(3), 253–264. https://doi.org/10.1007/s12402-011-0056-0

Gillette, H. (2022, May 4). *ADHD freeze: Understanding task paralysis*. Psych Central. https://psychcentral.com/adhd/adhd-paralysis

Hallowell, E., & M.D. (2023, March 28). *The benefits of ADHD support groups for adults, teens, and parents*. ADDitudemag. https://www.additudemag.com/your-add-life-adhd-support-groups/

Hardy, D. (2010). *The compound effect*. John Murray One.

Hassall, J. (2020). *Adult ADHD and emotions*. CHADD. https://chadd.org/attention-article/adult-adhd-and-emotions/#:

Hill, G. (2013, March 9). *Living with less. A lot less*. The New York Times. https://www.nytimes.com/2013/03/10/opinion/sunday/living-with-less-a-lot-less.html#:

Hutchinson, B. (2012, June 26). *Hyperfocus — at Your service*. ADDitude.

https://www.additudemag.com/hyperfocus-at-your-service/

jenna, knight. (2021, July 26). *Chunking: Breaking tasks into manageable parts*. Never Defeated Coaching. https://www.neverdefeatedcoaching.net/chunking-breaking-tasks-into-manageable-parts/

Keltner, D., & Marsh, J. (2015, January 8). *How gratitude beats materialism*. Greater Good. https://greatergood.berkeley.edu/article/item/materialism_gratitude_happiness

Kirgios, E. L., Mandel, G. H., Park, Y., Milkman, K. L., Gromet, D. M., Kay, J. S., & Duckworth, A. L. (2020, November). Teaching temptation bundling to boost exercise: A field experiment. *Organizational Behavior and Human Decision Processes, 161*, 20–35. https://doi.org/10.1016/j.obhdp.2020.09.003

Koltuska-Haskin, B. (2023, January 19). *How colors affect brain functioning*. Www.psychologytoday.com. https://www.psychologytoday.com/gb/blog/how-my-brain-works/202301/how-colors-affect-brain-functioning#:

Koseva, N. (2023, February 20). *ADHD emotional dysregulation*. The ADHD Centre. https://www.adhdcentre.co.uk/adhd-emotional-dysregulation/

Kruse, K. (2017, March 20). *How to increase your productivity with anchor habits*. Forbes. https://www.forbes.com/sites/kevinkruse/2017/03/20/how-to-increase-your-productivity-with-anchor-habits/#:

Lewis, J. (2016, July 13). *Binaural beats vs isochronic tones, which is more effective?* Mind Amend. https://www.mindamend.com/brainwave-entrainment/binaural-beats-vs-isochronic-tones/

Lewsley, J. (2021, August 30). *What to know about object permanence and adhd*. Medical News Today. https://www.medicalnewstoday.com/articles/object-permanence-adhd

Lindsay, E. K., Young, S., Smyth, J. M., Brown, K. W., & Creswell, J. D. (2018, January). Acceptance lowers stress reactivity: Dismantling mindfulness training in a randomized controlled trial. *Psychoneuroendocrinology, 87*, 63–73. https://doi.org/10.1016/j.psyneuen.2017.09.015

Littman, E. (2017, February 1). *Never enough? Why ADHD brains crave stimulation*. ADDitude. https://www.additudemag.com/brain-stimu

lation-and-adhd-cravings-dependency-and-regulation/

Livingstone, L. T., Coventry, W. L., Corley, R. P., Willcutt, E. G., Samuelsson, S., Olson, R. K., & Byrne, B. (2016, March 18). Does the environment have an enduring effect on ADHD? A longitudinal study of monozygotic twin differences in children. *Journal of Abnormal Child Psychology, 44*(8), 1487–1501. https://doi.org/10.1007/s10802-016-0145-9

Lovering, N. (2022, May 18). *ADHD and emotions: Relationship and tips to manage.* Healthline. https://www.healthline.com/health/adhd/emotional-regulation#:

Luman, M., Oosterlaan, J., & Sergeant, J. (2005, February). The impact of reinforcement contingencies on AD/HD: A review and theoretical appraisal. *Clinical Psychology Review, 25*(2), 183–213. https://doi.org/10.1016/j.cpr.2004.11.001

Mannino, E. (2022, May 31). *How to rewire your brain.* Center for Healthy Aging. https://www.research.colostate.edu/healthyagingcenter/2022/05/31/how-to-rewire-your-brain/#:

Matyjek, M., Meliss, S., Dziobek, I., & Murayama, K. (2020, August 19). A multidimensional view on social and non-social rewards. *Frontiers in Psychiatry, 11.* https://doi.org/10.3389/fpsyt.2020.00818

Mayo Clinic. (2019, June 22). *Adult Attention-Deficit/Hyperactivity Disorder (ADHD) - Symptoms and causes.* Mayo Clinic; Mayo Clinic. https://www.mayoclinic.org/diseases-conditions/adult-adhd/symptoms-causes/syc-20350878

McCoy, K. (2013, October 3). *Home cleaning tips for allergy sufferers.* EverydayHealth.com. https://www.everydayhealth.com/allergies/home-cleaning.aspx

McGilchrist, S. (2011, January 9). Music "releases mood-enhancing chemical in the brain." *BBC News.* https://www.bbc.co.uk/news/health-12135590#:

McMains, S., & Kastner, S. (2011, January 12). Interactions of top-down and bottom-up mechanisms in human visual cortex. *The Journal of Neuroscience, 31*(2), 587–597. https://doi.org/10.1523/JNEUROSCI.3766-10.2011

MedCircle. (2022, September 26). *The ADHD interest-based nervous system*. MedCircle. https://medcircle.com/articles/adhd-interest-based-nervous-system/#:

Mindful Staff. (2020, July 8). *What is mindfulness?* Mindful. https://www.mindful.org/what-is-mindfulness/

Mirzaei, N. (2022, March 2). *Binaural beats vs solfeggio frequencies: Which one is better?* Meditation Music Library. https://meditationmusiclibrary.com/blogs/wednesday-wisdom-blog/binaural-beats-vs-solfeggio-frequencies-which-one-is-better

Montijo, S. (2022, May 16). *How to declutter with ADHD*. Psych Central. https://psychcentral.com/adhd/ways-to-clear-out-clutter-when-you-have-adhd

Mwewa, M. (2023, May 17). *Anatomy of a habit: Cue, routine, and reward*. Kinnu. https://kinnu.xyz/kinnuverse/lifestyle/healthy-habits/the-anatomy-of-a-habit-cue-routine-and-reward/#:

National Institute of Mental Health. (2021). *NIMH» Attention-Deficit/Hyperactivity Disorder in adults: What you need to know*. Www.nimh.nih.gov. https://www.nimh.nih.gov/health/publications/adhd-what-you-need-to-know

NHS. (2018, November 20). *Mindfulness*. Nhs.uk. https://www.nhs.uk/mental-health/self-help/tips-and-support/mindfulness/

Nieminen, J. H., Asikainen, H., & Rämö, J. (2019). Promoting deep approach to learning and self-efficacy by changing the purpose of self-assessment: A comparison of summative and formative models. *Studies in Higher Education, 46*(7), 1–16. https://doi.org/10.1080/03075079.2019.1688282

Nigg, J. (2021, January 26). *How's your emotional resilience? Learning to cope with intense ADHD feelings*. ADDitude. https://www.additudemag.com/emotional-resilience-adhd-coping/

Objective of cleaning is not just to...Quote by "Marie Kondo" | What Should I Read Next? (n.d.). Www.whatshouldireadnext.com. https://www.whatshouldireadnext.com/quotes/marie-kondo-e215786f-1f0a-4ed8-8374-046f1e13f5ab-the-objective-of-cleaning-is

Osborne, J. B., Zhang, H., Carlson, M., Shah, P., & Jonides, J. (2023, July 27). The association between different sources of distraction and symptoms of attention deficit hyperactivity disorder. *Frontiers in*

Psychiatry, 14, 1173989. https://doi.org/10.3389/fpsyt.2023.1173989

Pangin, I. S. (2017, July 6). *7 relaxing colors and how they affect your mood!* The Times of India. https://timesofindia.indiatimes.com/life-style/health-fitness/de-stress/7-relaxing-colors-and-how-they-affect-your-mood/articleshow/46946305.cms#:

Park, M.-S., Byun, K.-W., Park, Y.-K., Kim, M.-H., Jung, S.-H., & Kim, H. (2013, April 25). Effect of complex treatment using visual and auditory stimuli on the symptoms of attention deficit/hyperactivity disorder in children. *Journal of Exercise Rehabilitation, 9*(2), 316–325. https://doi.org/10.12965/jer.130017

Pera, G. (2015, March 20). *ADHD, empathy, and dopamine - ADHD roller coaster with Gina Pera.* ADHD Roller Coaster. https://adhdrollercoaster.org/adhd-and-relationships/adhd-impaired-empathy-and-dopamine/

Phillips, H. (2023, January 12). *5 reasons a clean environment will improve your mental health.* CNET. https://www.cnet.com/health/mental/5-reasons-a-clean-space-will-improve-your-mental-health/

Philosophy, K. (n.d.). *Rule 6: Ask yourself if it sparks joy – KonMari | The Official Website of Marie Kondo.* Konmari.com. https://konmari.com/marie-kondo-rules-of-tidying-sparks-joy/

Pillay, S. (2016, May 16). *Greater self-acceptance improves emotional well-being.* Harvard Health Blog. https://www.health.harvard.edu/blog/greater-self-acceptance-improves-emotional-well-201605169546

Powers, S., Craig, W., Kohut, M., & Hallward, A. (2023, March 14). Narrative podcasts to foster empathy and reduce stigma among third-year medical students. *Academic Psychiatry.* https://doi.org/10.1007/s40596-023-01764-y

Rachael, G. (2022, August 6). *ADHD symptom spotlight: Overstimulation.* Verywell Mind. https://www.verywellmind.com/adhd-symptom-spotlight-overstimulation-5323859#:

Rattner, D. (2019, February 3). *How to use the psychology of space to boost your creativity.* Donald M. Rattner, Architect. https://donaldrattner.com/blog/2019/2/3/uybs7kgoti3ezjxrl6cb0u59fjwnqe

Saline, S. (2022, January 26). *ADHD hyperfocus: How to manage this double-edged sword for your health and productivity.* Dr. Sharon Saline. https://drsharonsaline.com/2022/01/26/adhd-hyperfocus-how-to-manage-this-double-edged-sword-for-your-health-and-productivity/

Saline, S., & Psy.D. (2022, February 15). *When perfectionism stems from ADHD: Challenging the fallacy of "not good enough."* ADDitude. https://www.additudemag.com/perfectionism-adhd-not-good-enough-anxiety/

Saxbe, D. E., & Repetti, R. (2009, November 23). No place like home: Home tours correlate with daily patterns of mood and cortisol. *Personality and Social Psychology Bulletin, 36*(1), 71–81. https://doi.org/10.1177/0146167209352864

Sedgwick, J. A., Merwood, A., & Asherson, P. (2018, October 29). The positive aspects of attention deficit hyperactivity disorder: a qualitative investigation of successful adults with ADHD. *ADHD Attention Deficit and Hyperactivity Disorders, 11*(11). https://doi.org/10.1007/s12402-018-0277-6

Seven benefits of following daily routines | Clockwise. (2022, November 26). Www.getclockwise.com. https://www.getclockwise.com/blog/benefits-daily-routines

Sherrell, Z. (2021, July 21). *What are the benefits of ADHD?* Www.medicalnewstoday.com. https://www.medicalnewstoday.com/articles/adhd-benefits

Silva, L. (2022, December 1). *The mental health benefits of a clean home.* Forbes Health. https://www.forbes.com/health/mind/mental-health-clean-home/#:

Sissons, B. (2023, May 23). *ADHD spectrum: Types, severity, diagnosis, and treatment.* Www.medicalnewstoday.com. https://www.medicalnewstoday.com/articles/adhd-spectrum#summary

Sreenivas, S. (2022, July 13). *How to organize your home with ADHD.* WebMD. https://www.webmd.com/add-adhd/tips-organize-home-adhd#:

Stanborough, R. J. (2020, April 1). *Benefits of music on body, mind, relationships & more.* Healthline. https://www.healthline.com/health/benefits-of-music

Stoler, D. (2023, February 15). *The many mental benefits of decluttering.* Www.psychologytoday.com. https://www.psychologytoday.com/gb/blog/the-resilient-brain/202302/the-many-mental-benefits-of-decluttering#:

Sutton, A. (2016). Measuring the effects of self-awareness: Construction of the self-awareness outcomes questionnaire. *Europe's Journal of Psychology, 12*(4), 645–658. NCBI. https://doi.org/10.5964/ejop.v12i4.1178

Swaim, E. (2022, May 2). *What's the connection between ADHD and self-esteem?* Healthline. https://www.healthline.com/health/adhd/adhd-and-self-esteem

Team, A. E. (2022, December 7). *ADHD paralysis is real: Here are 8 ways to overcome it.* ADDA - Attention Deficit Disorder Association. https://add.org/adhd-paralysis/

Therapy, E. Y. (2023, March 13). *How the reward system in ADHD affects motivation.* Embracing You Therapy. https://embracingyoutherapy.com/how-the-reward-system-in-adhd-affects-motivation/#:

Uvnäs-Moberg, K., & Petersson, M. (2005). Oxytocin, a mediator of anti-stress, well-being, social interaction, growth and healing. *Zeitschrift Für Psychosomatische Medizin Und Psychotherapie, 51*(1), 57–80. https://doi.org/10.13109/zptm.2005.51.1.57

Valmiki, M., Fawzy, P., Valmiki, S., Aid, M. A., Chaitou, A. R., Zahid, M., & Khan, S. (2021, March 5). Reinforcement and compensatory mechanisms in Attention-Deficit Hyperactivity Disorder: A systematic review of case-control studies. *Cureus, 5;13*(3) (:e13718). https://doi.org/10.7759/cureus.13718

Villines, Z. (2019, June 6). *Disordered executive function: Symptoms, causes, and treatment.* Www.medicalnewstoday.com. https://www.medicalnewstoday.com/articles/325402#:

Wang, S., & Aamodt, S. (2012, September-October). Play, stress, and the learning brain. *Cerebrum: The Dana Forum on Brain Science, 2012,* 12. https://www.ncbi.nlm.nih.gov/pmc/articles/PMC3574776/

Weintraub, K. (2019, March 25). *The human brain never stops growing neurons, a new study claims.* PBS NewsHour. https://www.pbs.org/

newshour/science/the-human-brain-never-stops-growing-neurons-a-new-study-claims

Westcott, Kyrus K. "10 Uplifting Quotes to Inspire Introverts with ADHD." LinkedIn. Last modified June 28, 2023. https://www.linkedin.com/pulse/10-uplifting-quotes-inspire-introverts-adhd-kyrus-keenan-westcott/.

Zanto, T. P., Johnson, V., Ostrand, A., & Gazzaley, A. (2022, October 3). How musical rhythm training improves short-term memory for faces. *Proceedings of the National Academy of Sciences, 119*(41). https://doi.org/10.1073/pnas.2201655119

Zenhabits. (2007, August 15). *A guide to creating a minimalist home.* Zen Habits. https://zenhabits.net/a-guide-to-creating-a-minimalist-home/

Made in United States
Troutdale, OR
07/30/2024